Washington D.C. Aug. 1966.

Adventures in
GREEK COOKERY

ADVENTURES

THE WORLD PUBLISHING COMPANY
Cleveland and New York

IN GREEK COOKERY

Stella Kopulos and Dorothy P. Jones

Illustrations by James Stewart

Published by The World Publishing Company
2231 West 110th Street, Cleveland, Ohio 44102
Published simultaneously in Canada by
Nelson, Foster & Scott Ltd.

FIRST EDITION

Library of Congress Catalog Card Number: 66–13150

Acknowledgments

MY FIRST debt of gratitude for making this book possible is to my parents, the late Chris and Mary Sianis, who engendered in me pride of our Greek heritage, an appreciation for good Greek food, and my basic knowledge of the cooking art.

Over the years many friends have contributed to this recipe collection and to some of the background information, but we are especially grateful to the following for their assistance during the preparation of the book: The Reverend James G. Kalaris, Pastor, Sts. Constantine and Helen Greek Orthodox Church, Washington, D.C.; Mr. John Varveris, Cantor, St. Sophia Greek Orthodox Cathedral, Washington, D.C., and his wife, Mrs. Sophia Varveris, an accomplished cook; Mrs. Vera Marick, Secretary, Greek Military Mission, Washington, D.C.; Mr. Mitchell Despotides, former Chef, Royal Greek Embassy, Washington, D.C.; Mr. John Danglis, noted chef, Athens; Mr. Sauren Jenazian, linguist and travel authority, Trans World Airlines, Athens, Greece.

—Stella Kopulos

Preface

COOKING HAS always proved a valuable auxiliary to diplomacy.
No one can question the importance that dinner parties have in
diplomatic life. Many a memorable international transaction has
been conducted around and between dinner tables. This is why
a preface by an ambassador's wife to a cookbook is not altogether
irrelevant.

Greek cooking, of which rich and varied recipes will be found
in this book, is obviously a very ancient art. It reflects the glories
as well as the vicissitudes of the Greek nation. It tells of victories,
conquests, and foreign occupations. Still it retains some general
characteristics that are closely connected with the soil of Greek
lands.

Many of the dishes that are the most popular in Greece bear
foreign names—Turkish, Persian, or Arabic. Those same dishes are
often found under slightly varied forms between Athens, the
Persian Gulf, and the Gulf of Bengal. Some came to Greece from
the East; others were exported from Greece to the Orient. Constantinople, in its days of Imperial Hellenism, was an unparalleled
center of luxury and refinement. The recipes of the cooks of Cleo-
patra or of Lucullus and Nero were used and tried in the kitchens

of the Emperors and of the Greek grandees. To these delicacies were added all those that conquerors or merchants gathered in Babylon or Venice. When the Turks conquered Constantinople, they found and adopted, among other luxuries and amenities of the great Capital, a treasure of cooking alchemy. This is why a good many of the excellent dishes that this book presents bear Turkish names.

It is, however, interesting to observe that the main ingredients of Greek cooking are indigenous to Greece proper. They are not, as a rule, spices and condiments from exotic lands. Olive oil, oregano, thyme, laurel leaves, cloves, pistachio nuts, pignolia nuts, currants, and all the fragrant herbs of the Greek countryside figure prominently in Greek cooking. Honey is, to this day, the main condiment of many Greek pastries and sweetmeats. The resin, which is an indispensable ingredient of some Greek wines, is commemorated in ancient Greek figurative art by the fir cone that surmounts the orgiastic stick of the Bacchae, companions of Dionysos, god of wine.

All these are evidence that a good deal of the Greek recipes are of very ancient origin; and that they were devised before Hellenism reached its two imperial phases of the conquest of Alexander the Great and the Byzantine Empire.

Unfortunately, one rarely cares, while eating something, about its historical origin or associations; therefore this preface has less value than any of the recipes of this book. I should let them speak to the palate of the readers. I only wanted to remind them that some of the dishes that they will try might well have figured at the symposium of Plato, the banquet of Trimalcio in Rome, or under the tent of Heraclius the Great advancing toward Babylon.

Mrs. Alexander A. Matsas

Royal Greek Embassy
Washington, D.C.
December, 1965

Contents

As sorrowful, yet always rejoicing;
as poor, yet making many rich;
as having nothing, and yet
possessing all things.

II CORINTHIANS, 6:10

Introduction

MY INTRODUCTION to Greek food occasioned also an introduction to my co-author, Stella Kopulos. The time was Greek Easter Week, 1961. In the Parish Hall of Sts. Constantine and Helen Greek Orthodox Church in Washington, D.C., along with more than one hundred other non-Greeks, I enjoyed a Greek Easter Dinner and an authentic sampling of modern Hellenic culture. Greek Easter foods elaborately match the joyous and spectacular celebration of this, the greatest of all festive times. The delicious food is only one element of a whole atmosphere which includes singing, dancing, wine-toasting, and the sacred grandeur of Orthodox liturgy and religious art.

Stella Kopulos was the cook who prepared that magnificent meal and is the first of many Greeks I have come to know both in America and in Greece. Their warm hospitality has led me on what I can only describe as a grand gourmet tour and education in modern Greek culture.

Mrs. Kopulos has spent most of her life interpreting Greek culture to Americans by capitalizing on her greatest talent, cooking. She has perfected it to a fine art since first becoming a helper in her father's Kansas City restaurant at age eight. Her efforts serve a dual purpose as she creates international understanding and goodwill while also raising money for charity institutions in Greece. She knows American taste, for she has lived in this country since age five, but being Greek-born, Greek-speaking, and a frequent traveler to Greece, she continues to feel the pulse of her native land.

Following World War II, the fascist occupation, and communist guerrilla warfare, concern for relatives in Greece and an awareness of the desperate needs of the people aroused Mrs. Kopulos, her family, and friends to find ways to help. Living then in Washington, D. C., she undertook a variety of money-raising activities in order to send help to the Greeks. She first returned to her homeland in 1955 to visit the schools, hospitals, and child-care centers receiving assistance through her efforts.

Realizing that help of the scope she hoped to give the Greeks could only be provided by large organizations, Mrs. Kopulos engaged clubwomen of America in her cause. Promoting the distribution of Greek-made products, she has found a ready market at women's club conventions where she also sells Greek sweets and other delicacies from her own kitchen. Her very significant contribution in international welfare work was recognized by the American Mothers' Committee in 1962 when she was named International Mother of the Year. The same year, under the sponsorship of the District of Columbia Business and Professional Women's Club, she was selected District of Columbia Mother of the Year.

While touring rural areas of Greece to visit the various institutions she is concerned with, Mrs. Kopulos established a rapport with villagers who opened their hearts to her in gratitude. She learned firsthand their ways of domestic life. Her natural interest in cookery resulted in a collection of their recipes which she combines with her other favorites for this book.

Because few Greek cooks use written recipes, it is difficult to gain precise information from them. Mrs. Kopulos has watched them cook, tasted the results, and then cooked her way through literally tons of ingredients to adapt and record their recipes for American cooks. Recognizing that taste preferences and digestive tolerance for certain foods are influenced by environment and habit, she has modified the recipes to suit American taste, for many Greek foods are extremely heavy or excessively oily. Making use of our many electrical appliances and other conveniences is a departure from the Greek method, but she does not feel it destroys authentic character and may improve results.

The selection of dishes is extremely varied in order to illustrate the many characteristics of this national cuisine. Some are simple or humble, others exotic or elegant. There are traditional specialties, some of contemporary style, and some flexible instructions to stimulate creative cookery in the Greek manner.

In joining Mrs. Kopulos in preparation of this book, I do so not as another expert cook, which I am not, but rather as one fascinated with the Greek cuisine and its related food lore. My new familiarity with Greek cookery has made my everyday cooking more interesting. Guests have been intrigued with some of the more unusual dishes which never fail to interject an interesting conversational element to parties. May your cooking become more exciting also as you learn to cook in the Greek manner.

—Dorothy P. Jones

Scarsdale, New York
December, 1965

1 · Meeting the Greeks

JUST AS we become better acquainted with a new-found friend when we are invited to his home for a meal, so too we can come to know the Greek people by exploring their cookery and food lore.

Greek cookery reveals a nation's way of life, for through it the people express their patriotism, religious devotion, loves, joys, sorrows, thankfulness, and warm hospitality. There are foods to celebrate the joy of birth or to mourn the dead, to seek good luck, or to thank a protective patron saint. The Greeks hail Christ's Resurrection with red-dyed eggs and recall His suffering on the Cross with vinegar-soured soup. Ancient religious and social customs as well as superstitions play a part in the food lore, making many special foods so much an integral part of the life of the people that they could not disappear unless modern Greek culture also died. The full expressiveness of Greek cookery can be appreciated only in conjunction with the full year's calendar of events and the related foods.

Like every national cuisine, the food of the Greeks reflects history and geographic environment, economic development and prosperity, social and religious mores, foreign influences, and refinements of culture, as well as man's own creativeness applied to food preparation. There is an evolutionary process to cookery from century to century and from decade to decade. We see a parallel development with Greek food as we look from peasant village, to progressive town, to Athens, where the food evolves from simple nourishment, to tasty variety, to gastronomic delight.

Greece is an agricultural country producing a wide variety of food crops on the varied terrain. However, because eighty percent of the land is too mountainous to be tillable, food supplies are limited and often inadequate. Greek cookery is very practical, always making the most of what is on hand. Food processing as an industry is still in its infancy in Greece. There is little refrigeration except in the larger towns and cities. Every edible item finds respectable use, as for example, lamb's head and entrails, which are used for very special dishes. Seasonal products which cannot be preserved are used so generously as to seem extravagant, but this is the Greek way of avoiding spoilage and waste. The laws of nature produce this feast or famine condition with food supplies, but the Greek Orthodox Church contributes order and meaning to it through the discipline of fasting.

A traveler in Greece is constantly aware of the force of religion in daily life, for the church calendar takes precedence in scheduling both public and private activity. Among the devout, about two hundred days of the year are observed with some degree of fasting. This was true for everyone a few decades ago, but the practice has been relaxed by some in recent years.

In the strict pattern, every Wednesday and Friday is a meatless day (including vertebrate fish), as are the forty days before Christmas. During the forty-eight days of Lent in the Orthodox calendar, all animal products, including milk, cheese, eggs, and butter, are omitted from the diet. Fish is allowed on Palm Sunday, but the diet is even more restricted during Holy Week. On

Good Friday the only food permitted is the special bean or lentil soup seasoned with vinegar, a solemn tradition recalling that vinegar was given Christ on the Cross when He thirsted.

The fifteen days preceding Assumption Day from August 1 to 15 is another fast period called Small Lent. Three other days observed as fast days are the Eve of Epiphany on January 5, Holy Cross Day on September 14, and the Day of the Beheading of St. John the Baptist on August 29.

Holidays are great occasions with much merriment and feasting—no wonder when the people practice so much self-denial!

Many foods have regional character, a fact emphasizing how much peasant life and folkways can differ among people living only a few dozen miles apart. The rugged mountain terrain of the mainland creates barriers that divide the land regionally, keeping some areas quite isolated. A mountaineer herdsman, seaside fisherman, or farmer of the plains is each individualistic, patriotic to his own locality, and inherently rooted to the primitive way of life of generations before him. Traces of foreign influence, sometimes many centuries old, are still identifiable in the cooking of some areas. In Macedonia it is an influence from other Balkan countries, and where Albanians settled, as on the island of Salamis, their influence has survived. Italian influence lingers in some of the islands of the Cyclades where Venetians settled at the time of the Crusades.

The most general penetration of foreigners occurred after the Turks gained domination in 1453 and Greece became part of the Ottoman Empire. Moslem Turks and Greeks lived side by side, but even after four hundred years of commingling, their cultures remained disparate. Some similarities inevitably emerged, the most apparent being in cookery. Common characteristics, such as the manner of barbecue-grilling meats, and making the rich, flaky, honey-soaked pastries such as Baklava, are considered today as much Greek as Turkish.

Foreign influences have resulted also from Greeks themselves reaching out to new horizons and returning home with new ideas. The Greeks have always been a cosmopolitan people, looking both east and west as their land delineates the two cultural spheres. They colonized throughout the Mediterranean and Asia Minor long before Alexander the Great conquered and spread Hellenism through the Middle East to India, the Balkans, North Africa, and the Western Mediterranean.

When the Roman Empire conquered and enveloped the Greek World, Greek learning and culture were carried to Rome and became the foundation of the new order. Christianity spread rapidly among the Greeks, and Greek missionaries established the Church in the Balkans and in Russia, ties that remained firm after the Church split into eastern and western branches in 1054.

When the captial of the empire was moved to Constantinople in the early fourth century, the Byzantine Era was born. The Church and Byzantine culture developed almost as one, becoming more and more foreign to the West. Greeks became less eastern, however, with the rise of Islam, for the militant push of the Moslems forced them out of Asia, back to the Balkan Peninsula and to a few small islands. During the years of Turkish rule, the Greek Orthodox Church was a unifying ethnic force and to this day is completely interwoven into all Greek life.

The Greeks possess an indomitable spirit that has survived the hardships of poverty, war, and occupation. Intensely proud of their heritage, they individually display dignity and self-respect, even in the most humble circumstances. If a man is poor he feels no disgrace, for poverty has been the plague of many generations. Class distinction is probably of less concern to the Greek than to any other European.

Since winning freedom in 1829, Greeks have affirmed their independence with a dogged determination to remain free. Every October 28 they observe Okhi Day, a national holiday commemorating Greek resistance to attack by the fascists in 1940. "Okhi" means "No," their firm answer when invited to surrender to the invading forces. On a mountainside above the city of Tripolis in the Peloponnesus, the Greeks spelled out their answer in huge letters of white asbestos that stand out against the brown hillside. The fighting was savage and the Greeks suffered hardships and atrocities while seeing their country desecrated. But surrender? Never!

OKHI is as prominently visible on the mountainside today, for the white asbestos is replenished annually by soldiers of the national barracks located in the city below. It stands out for miles around as a symbol of the spirit of the Greek people.

The Greek character seems to have been strongly tempered by two schools of philosophy from the earlier culture. From Stoicism, the Hellene derived an enduring strength to meet challenges and hardships, and from Epicurianism he developed a zest for life which he displays with gay abandon. Elements of his pagan past have survived to be molded into the Christian pattern. His patron saints, for example, are much like the protective gods of ancient times.

Greece is a small country with a population of only 8,500,000. Her people have migrated to many parts of the world as the homeland is too poor and meagerly productive to feed the population adequately. About 1,500,000 Americans are of Greek descent, and several million other Greeks have settled around the world. Everywhere they share the same pride of heritage and respect for Greek traditions. Greeks who migrated did so, not to escape their Greek background, but rather to find a more favorable economic climate in which to continue being themselves. Wherever Greek immigrants have gone, the Orthodox Church has gone also to become the center of life in the new Greek community and to keep alive the Greek language as well as religious and social customs. Many Greeks have retained close ties with the homeland, especially if relatives remained behind. It is not unusual for elderly people to return to their native villages to live out their lives after spending their working years abroad.

The first Greek-Americans remained isolated in their ethnic group, but succeeding generations have broadened their interests and activities. Enterprise and talent have produced considerable wealth among them, but still the Greek spirit survives and finds compatibility with twentieth-century American life. With a well of enthusiasm, boundless energy, and generous hearts, the Greeks spare nothing to give an occasion its appropriate grandeur. Be it a wedding, baptism, or other great moment—it deserves their full expression and nothing less will do.

2 · Special Times for Feasting

FOURTEEN LEGAL holidays are observed in Greece during the year, all religious days except the strictly patriotic Okhi Day on October 28. National Independence Day, March 25, coincides with Annunciation Day, making it a religious as well as patriotic holiday. Name days, weddings, and baptisms are occasions for special celebration, and solemn memorial observances commemorate the dead. A behind-the-scenes look at food preparations for many of these days reveals the occasion itself.

Greeks look for signs of good luck as they usher in the New Year. Card games and gambling are the favorite pastime of New Year's Eve. At midnight, in many households, family and friends gather around the table for the ceremonial cutting of the Vasilopita or New Year's bread. Even the children are awakened for the event, one they look forward to with excitement, because a coin is baked in the bread to bring good luck for the coming year to the one who gets it in his slice. The head of the house slices the bread, putting the first piece aside designated for the house, for the Holy Mother, or for St. Basil, the patron saint of the day.

If the coin is in this slice it means good luck for everyone. The next slice is for the father, next the mother, then the children, eldest first, then relatives and friends. Whatever is left is sent to the poor the next day, and alas! it may still have the coin. As customs vary among families or in different regions, the bread is served by some at the New Year's Day meal, sliced in the same way.

The tradition is observed in many Greek-American homes as well as at Greek Orthodox Churches in this country. Every parish holds an annual Vasilopita Feast the Sunday evening following New Year's Day, with sufficient loaves to cut slices for all the parishoners. The feasts are fund-raising events to benefit St. Basil's Academy in Garrison, New York, a Greek Orthodox religious training school and orphanage.

A roasting chicken, turkey, or lamb is usually served at the New Year's Day meal, accompanied by pilaf, the grains of rice symbolizing prosperity for the coming year. Kourambiethes, Melomakarouna, and Baklava are popular sweets for the day.

New Year's Day, rather than Christmas, is the time for exchanging gifts. It is also the time of many festive open-house parties, for the men named Basil (and there are many) celebrate their name day by entertaining all their friends. Guests are served a variety of liquors as well as coffee and an assortment of hors d'oeuvres and sweets.

Epiphany Day, January 6, follows a fast day and is a special day of feasting to commemorate Christ's baptism. On the island of Amigos a special sweet for this day is Loukoumades, a fried syrup-dipped goodie of very ancient origin.

In most of Greece, Loukoumades are particularly associated with March 9, the Day of Forty Martyrs, when housewives make forty Loukoumades to remember the forty saints.

Anticipating the long austere period of Lent which lasts for forty-eight days in the Orthodox Church, the Greeks celebrate Carnival Time for two weeks preceeding Clean Monday, the first day of Lent. They are very gay with dancing, masquerading, and parading with floats. It is a time for good eating, especially of the foods from which they will abstain during Lent. The weather is cool and invigorating, whetting appetites for rich foods and sweets. The tender spring lamb is popular throughout the time of Carnival, but it is a special feature of the menu for Meat Fare Sunday, the second Sunday before Lent. Cheese Eating Week follows when the perishable milk products and eggs are all consumed, and the climactic day is Cheese Fare Sunday, the last day of Carnival feasting. This is a family day with special foods and activities. Macaroni and cheese is always served and Svingous, a fried sweet puff, is the usual dessert. The last item on the Carnival table is eggs, appearing again as the first food on the Easter table. The eggs are often baked in outdoor wood fires, each person writing his name on an egg and placing it in the wood ashes to cook.

Fasting begins on Clean Monday when the Greeks eat only seafood and vegetables as well as Lagana, a traditional unleavened bread prepared for this day. Lagana is made of flour, salt, and water kneaded with a little oil, then sprinkled with sesame seeds before baking. It must be eaten while hot before it cools and hardens, and is often spread with Greek caviar and served with black olives. Clean Week which follows is a sort of spring house-cleaning time when villagers whitewash their houses.

During the seven weeks of Lent the diet includes only vegetables, fruit, bread, olives, and invertebrate seafoods. The fast is relaxed on Independence Day, however, when fish and a limited quantity of sweets are allowed. On Palm Sunday there is another slackening of the fast and various fish dishes are the popular fare for the dinner meal with Halvah or Melomakarouna for dessert. Holy Week is most austere, and on Good Friday nothing is eaten except lentil or bean soup seasoned with vinegar.

Easter, still calculated by the Orthodox Church according to the Julian Calendar, is the most festive time of the year. The celebration begins at midnight Easter Eve and continues throughout Easter Week. Joyous cries of "Christos Anesti" ("Christ has

Risen") spread the news of Resurrection among all who attend midnight church services. The first Easter meal follows during the early morning hours when red-dyed eggs and Mayiritsa, a soup made of the entrails of the paschal lamb, are served. Family members crack eggs together, each person holding a hard-boiled red egg in his hand and tapping it against another's, attempting to crack the other person's while keeping his own unbroken.

For the Easter Day meal whole lambs are cooked on spits over outdoor fires. Everyone, even the very poor, has lamb for Easter. In many towns and villages the cooking of the lambs is a community activity with crowds gathering to sing, dance, and drink wine while the men take turns hand-turning the spits. The feast includes Kouloura, the Easter bread baked with a red egg in the center, Tyropita (cheese tarts,) and yogurt. Salad, vegetables, cheese, and olives are part of the menu as well as Koulourakia, the traditional Easter cookies that are coated with sesame seeds.

The supplies of eggs and dairy products that have accumulated during Lent are used generously in the Easter foods, making them very rich. The rich foods, especially many sweets, are served until the weather turns hot. During the summer months the many kinds of delicious fresh fruit that grow in Greece are favored over sweets, even for special occasions.

Assumption Day on August 15 follows two weeks of fasting and is another occasion for special feasting. A suckling pig is often cooked over an outdoor fire for this holiday.

After forty days of fasting between November 15 and December 24, the Greeks also celebrate Christmas with special foods. Christopsomo is the special Christmas bread and the popular holiday cookies, Kourambiethes, are usually served. Lamb is a favorite meat for the day, for this is the time of year when the young lambs are just ready for slaughter, but turkey and roast chicken are other choices.

Greeks pay little attention to birthdays, but rather celebrate the passing of a year on the saint's day for whom the person was named. Those with names of other origin celebrate on All Saints' Day. If a saint's day falls during Lent, the celebration is postponed until the day following Easter.

Throughout Greece there are hundreds of tiny chapels, each dedicated to a particular saint. Empty and unused the rest of the year, on the particular saint's day they become the scene of celebration for all in the area named for the saint. Families accompany the namesake, bringing a basket meal, to spend the day sharing in festivities.

In the cities, name day observances are more formal, especially among the prosperous. Women observe the day within the family, perhaps with a dinner for relatives and close friends. For the man of the house, however, a large open house is held for all friends and neighbors. The custom is so taken for granted, even among Greek-Americans, that families not planning such an event find it necessary to announce the fact in church so they will not be overwhelmed with callers.

The King's Name Day, the Feast of Sts. Constantine and Helen on May 21, is a national holiday when all the country joins in celebration with festivals, religious processions, and folk dancing at the churches dedicated to the first Christian emperor and his mother.

Cities and towns also observe the days of their patron saints with celebrations which sometimes last several days. Salonica's patron saint is St. Demetrius, and a three-day holiday begins there on October 26. It is the first great festival of the winter season and it coincides with the time of opening and tasting the new wine. St. Andrew's Day is observed by the people of Patras with celebrations and processions on November 30. Corfu honors St. Spyridon with a three-day celebration reaching a climax on his day, December 13.

Weddings in Greece are solemn rituals without the elaborate adornments Americans associate with such an event. Following the ceremony, however, the mood changes to robust gaiety when the bride's father is host to all in the community. Dancing and celebrating may continue for two or three days. It is still the custom to provide a dowry for a girl, and the sons of the family share in this responsibility, not marrying themselves until their sisters are wed.

Weddings are never held during Lent. Villagers usually plan weddings during the warm months so that festivities can be held out of doors. Everyone is served food and wine, the quantity and elaborateness depending on the means of the bride's father. Koufeta, a commercially made candy, is the traditional wedding candy. It is made of sugar-coated whole almonds, wrapped in white tulle, and distributed to all the guests. Lamb, wine, and sweets—especially Kourambiethes, the powdered sugar crescent cookies—are usually served. More elaborate feasts include a variety of hors d'oeuvres and many sweets. Other liquors, such as masticha and ouzo, may supplement several kinds of wine. Well-to-do Athenians give large and very elaborate wedding dinners after the church ceremony.

Religion plays an important part in the personal life of every Greek, and the baptism of a baby is one of the most significant events of life, taking place sometime between the sixth week and sixth month after birth. Godparents assume their role with devotion and a high sense of responsibility, vowing to watch over the child until he is thirteen years old. Relatives and friends are present to rejoice in the child's birth into the Christian fold, and receive as a memento a small medallion of the Christ Child and Virgin which has been provided by the godparents. Sometimes Koufeta, wrapped in pastel tulle rather than white, also is distributed.

Following the church service, the parents entertain in their home with either a reception or dinner. It may be a simple affair where only cookies and a drink are served (usually Kourambiethes and masticha or ouzo) or it may be lavish with many hors d'oeuvres and sweets as well as a variety of drinks. Often there is dancing.

There is deep mourning in a family during the first forty days after a death. Following the funeral service and during the forty-day period, callers in the home are served only Greek coffee or cognac and non-sweet Paximade, a Greek toast which resembles Zwieback. A special memorial food called Koliva is prepared on the ninth day, the fourtieth day, at the end of the third and the sixth months, and one year after death. It is taken to church and placed on a table in front of the altar during the memorial service. It then is spooned into little bags and distributed to the congregation after the service. Made from boiled wheat germ symbolizing Resurrection, Koliva also contains parsley, sesame seeds, pomegranate seeds, and raisins. The mixture is piled in a solid mass on a tray and generously covered with powdered sugar. It is edged with almonds and the outline of a cross is made in the center with small candies. The initials of the departed person are outlined on each side of the cross in black raisins. The three Saturdays preceding the first Saturday of Lent are called Memorial Saturdays when all the departed are remembered and hundreds of trays of Koliva are brought to the church.

3 · Characteristics of
Greek Cookery

OUR MODERN kitchen equipment and wide assortment of packaged and frozen foods would seem unbelievable to most Greek peasant wives, for they are still living in primitive surroundings. A peasant kitchen is no more than a tiny cupboard and iron pot hanging in the fireplace. Water is carried from a well, and perishable foods are stored in a screen box hung inside the well in summer to keep cool. Baking is done in an outside oven, a huge mound of mud looking much like a giant beehive. In the larger villages housewives send their food to be baked in a community oven tended by a professional baker. His job is strictly mechanical and the food preparation must be done at home.

Meals are simple in village homes with such limited facilities. A combination of foods are cooked together in a single pot as a soup or stew. Bread and olives are the basis of the diet. From goats' milk the Greeks make cheese and yogurt. There are fresh fruits and vegetables in season and grapes to make wine. If they live near the sea there will be lots of fish, but meat is an infrequent luxury, enjoyed by some only at Easter. Dried products such as rice, macaroni, beans, and salt fish supplement the diet when fresh produce is unavailable. During the summer months, village cooks prepare a supply of Hilopites (homemade noodles) and Trahana, a mealy substance of noodle character, to be used during the winter. The diet is a healthy one, but it is monotonous. In sharp contrast to the drabness of everyday life, holidays with their gaiety are times for good eating, and village cooks can produce some excellent dishes, even with their limited facilities.

Economic conditions have been easing during the last decade, giving the villagers a little money with which to buy a greater variety of foods. Generally though, Greek women resist change for they are ever-conscious of the traditions and superstitions related to food.

The most striking change will be apparent as the present generation of youths reaches adulthood, for opportunities are open to them never afforded previous generations. Their expanded outlook grows out of educational and vocational training. Schools established by the Royal family, the Greek government, and other agencies are equipped by CARE and other aid sources with modern facilities to teach food preparation and canning. As the housewives and mothers of tomorrow, these students will certainly inaugurate a new era in Greek village homemaking.

In contrast to the villages, modern Athens is a thriving metropolis where the old patterns of life are streamlined and Europeanized. Though many hotels catering to European and American tourists serve primarily non-Greek food, cooking in the homes of the city is done in the traditional Greek manner. Excellent Greek food is served in many good restaurants and the famous tavernes of the city. A trip to Athens would not be complete without spending an evening in the convivial atmosphere of a taverna where a vast array of specialties is offered, as well as good Greek wine. The patisseries tempt one with their mouth-watering displays of rich pastries, cookies, cakes, and candies. On the streets, vendors sell typical Greek snacks such as sesame rolls, candies, hot chestnuts, pistachio nuts, and passa tempo (roasted melon seeds). Travelers find Souvlakia (charcoal-grilled bits of meat) for sale in all the stations and train stops. At the many sidewalk cafés where Greeks frequently stop for leisurely visiting and some refreshment, "mezedes," or "a bite to eat," are served along with a cup of coffee, glass of ouzo, wine, beer, or soft drink.

A Greek-American's interpretation of Greek cookery falls somewhere between village simplicity and Athenian elegance. All Greek cooks are creative, improvising and making variations as their supplies suggest. Knowing foods, their many possible uses and compatible combinations, comes from experience. An acquaintance with the Greeks' way with food should give American cooks inspiration for their own cooking creativeness.

Olive oil, onion, garlic, lemon, honey, cheese, wine, and a wide variety of herbs are the basic seasonings that give Greek food its character. Foods cooked in combinations, as meat and vegetables together, diffuse into delightful flavor blends. Mingled flavors are also achieved with marinades and sauces. Among the more elegant Greek foods are those made with Avgolemono Sauce, a delicate combination of egg, lemon juice, and the cooking stock from the food with which the sauce is to be served. This sauce is served over hot dolmades (meat-stuffed grape leaves) and stuffed eggplant, and is incorporated in some soups and stews but is not served with vegetables alone. Dishes with this sauce never contain tomatoes as they are not compatible. If wine is included in the recipe it must be dry white wine. The sauce requires careful though not difficult preparation to avoid curdling, and the dish must be served at once. Because the sauce varies in consistency and tartness according to the requirements of each dish, this book does not include a separate Avgolemono Sauce recipe but rather gives specific quantities of ingredients and instructions each time Avgolemono Sauce appears.

The Greek countryside produces many herbs which are used both fresh and dry. Oregano, dill, parsley, mint, rosemary, marjoram, thyme, bay leaves, cumin, and anise seeds—all familiar herbs to us—are used extensively by the Greeks. Cinnamon, nutmeg, and cloves are common to them also, and some unusual flavorings are used in cookies and cakes. Masteha, a gum sap from the same source as masticha, the apéritif, is used in some breads and cookies. Mahlepe, a seed from Syria, is used in the New Year's bread. Orange flower water and rose water are flavorings for some cookies and candies. Sesame seeds are sprinkled over breads and the Easter cookies, Koulourakia.

Having the just-right touch with seasonings is what makes one a gourmet cook. The results should be distinctive but not overpowering, and with experience one can develop a "seasoning thumb."

Onion appears in most Greek dishes using meat, vegetables, fish, and poultry, but garlic is generally used sparingly in recipes. A garlic sauce called Skordalia is popular, however, on many kinds of fish, beets, fried zucchini, fried eggplant, and braised rabbit.

Olive oil, an abundant product in Greece, is an essential staple used in every type of dish, even some desserts. Its distinctive taste makes it a fundamental element of flavoring. Meats and vegetables are often sautéed first in the oil before liquid is added for the remainder of cooking. Olive oil is always used over fresh salads or cooked greens. Because Americans often object to excessive use of oil, the quantity is minimized in the recipes in this book and vegetable oil is sometimes substituted.

Lemon agrees with almost all foods, and the Greeks use it extensively, not only for benefit of its tangy flavor, but because it has magical qualities as well. Lemon juice is squeezed over boiled vegetables after they are cooked. Before meats are cooked they are often seasoned and sprinkled with lemon juice to tenderize them. A few drops in syrup will prevent it from crystallizing when kept at room temperature, and will keep a stiffly beaten meringue from falling.

Wine is as much a food as an alcoholic beverage to the Greeks.

Some excellent wines are produced in the country for commercial distribution, but there is also a great deal of homemade wine of varying quality. Grapes grow nearly everywhere, and families that do not make their own wine supply can buy it very cheaply. Greek wine has rich nutritional value and is served to children as well as adults. Meat is often marinated in wine before cooking. Wine is added to many fish, poultry, vegetable, and meat dishes to enhance flavor. Dry wines are best for these, but sweet wines are used in cakes and cookies, acting as a preservative as well as flavoring.

Greek cheese is made from sheep or goat milk, the most popular being feta, a soft, white, and very crumbly cheese which is rather salty. It is an all-purpose cheese which is good in salads, with bread or crackers, and for cooking. Feta is available in this country wherever imported food products are sold. Kasseri is a deluxe white cheese, milder and less salty than feta, and firmer as it is richer in butter fat. Because it is expensive, it is served with hot bread rather than used in cooking. Kefalotyri is a strong-flavored, hard, and salty cheese which is generally used grated like Parmesan or Romano on spaghetti, meats, and soups. Those who prefer the milder flavor can substitute either of these for kefalotyri when grated cheese is called for. The Greeks also make a soft pot cheese called myzithra, but being highly perishable, it is not available here. There are many local cheeses which are identified by other names, but they are basically the same as one or another of those mentioned.

Milk is made into yogurt as well as cheese. Thicker than the commercially made yogurt in this country, it is eaten plain or as a topping for pilaf. Many families put a bowl on the table for every meal, and the Easter feast is not complete without yogurt. It is a rather recent practice to use it as a recipe ingredient, and the homemaking schools of Greece have developed some excellent recipes which we include in this book.

Beehives are everywhere, but the honey varies in quality and flavor depending on the local wild flowers. In some mountain areas where there is an abundance of heather, it has a strong flavor which we find objectionable. The honey from Mt. Hymettus in Attica, however, is one of the best in the world. A flower honey, it is full-bodied and a little darker than our American clover honey.

Flaky pastries are made from fillo, a pastry dough stretched into sheets as thin as tissue paper and then used in many layers, each brushed with melted butter. Besides the dessert pastries, fillo is used also for non-sweet pastries filled with a cheese, spinach, meat, or poultry mixture. These are served as hors d'oeuvres, a starter course at dinner, or for a luncheon entrée, and can be made in individual triangles or as a large sheet to be cut in individual pieces.

In spite of their interest in good food, many Greeks are quite indifferent to the temperature at which it is served. This shortcoming derives from the awkwardness of their facilities, but because it is a general attitude, restaurants put little stress on serving food hot. Somewhat in defense of the attitude, however, there are some baked dishes which improve in texture if allowed to set firmly before serving, especially those containing custard, such as Moussaka, Pastichio, and Cheese Pie. Meats will carve easier, too, if they are removed from the oven a while before slicing. A little reheating in a slow oven is always possible just before serving.

HORS D'OEUVRES

SERVED COLD:

ELIES MARINATA *[Marinated Olives]*
YIALANDJI DOLMADAKIA *[Stuffed Grape Leaves (Meatless)]*
RENGHA *[Smoked Herring]*
TYRI OREKTIKO *[Cheese Spread]*

SERVED HOT:

TARAMOKEFTEDES *[Tarama Balls]*
MEEKRA KEFTEDAKIA *[Small Meat Balls with Sauce]*
TIGANITO TYRI *[Fried Cheese Squares]*
TIGANITA SIKOTAKIA *[Fried Chicken Livers]*
KALAMARAKIA *[Squid]*
GEARAKIA *[Fried Lamb Sundries]*
KOKORETSI *[Grilled Lamb Sundries]*
TYROPITAKIA *[Cheese-filled Triangles]*
SPANAKOPITAKIA *[Spinach-filled Triangles]*
KREATOPITAKIA *[Meat-filled Triangles]*
HIRINO KRASSATO *[Pork Cooked in Wine]*

4 · Hors D'Oeuvres

MEZEDAKIA is the Greek word for hors d'oeuvres, shortened simply to mezedes when referring to a bite to eat. They may be elaborate or as simple as olives, cheese, nuts, and pieces of meat or fish.

"Come for mezedakia," is an invitation for the late afternoon social hour. Unlike the American cocktail hour, the focus is on the food specialties rather than on the accompanying drinks. Athenians dine very late and appease their late-afternoon appetites with satisfying snacks. The hors d'oeuvres, which are often hot, are served on small individual plates and some require the use of a fork.

Certain hors d'oeuvres are also served as the first course at dinner, are among the assortment of foods for a buffet table, and are served in late evening in the tavernes to after-theater patrons.

In addition to the cooked hors d'oeuvres there are other Greek specialities for this purpose which require no preparation and are available in stores that carry imported foods. We suggest trying Salonika peppers, marinated mixed vegetables, and miniature eggplants which are no more than two inches long. These all come in glass jars. Greek anchovies, octopus, and lakerda fillets are available in cans. The last, a delicacy from the Black Sea, is a little like bonita or tuna.

Tarama is Greek caviar, orange-pink in color, which can be purchased in jars. Besides using it for the fried Tarama Balls, we suggest the Taramosalata (Caviar Salad) in Chapter 6 as a spread for crackers at cocktail time.

Feta cheese and olives are such staples in a Greek home that they appear on the dinner table regularly as well as being served as mezedakia. The most popular of the Greek eating olives is the Kalamata, a large black, pointed, and slit olive cured with vinegar. There are many varieties of Greek olives treated in different ways for different purposes. Those which are salted should be used only for cooking, but unfortunately they are sometimes used as table olives and give a mistaken impression of Greek olives.

There is a conspicuous lack of pickles, as we know them, among the assortment of Greek hors d'oeuvres. Otherwise the assortment is broad and contributes justifiably to the fame of Greek cookery.

SERVED COLD

ELIES MARINATA

[Marinated Olives]

This is an old family recipe developed to give American olives a Greek flavor. Use Kalamatas if they are available for they are especially good prepared this way.

1 pound large black olives (about 1 quart)
3 stalks celery, from center of head, finely chopped
3 cloves garlic, finely chopped
1 lemon, cut in small pieces
juice of 2 lemons
1 cup olive oil

1½ cups wine vinegar
2 tablespoons oregano

Drain the olives and slit one side of each with a knife to allow the marinade to penetrate. This is not necessary for Kalamatas, which have a natural slit. Combine the olives with all other ingredients and pack in jars. If the liquid does not completely cover the olives, add water to cover. Seal and allow to marinate 2 to 3 weeks before serving. Shake the jars every few days. The olives will keep well in this marinade for six months.

YIALANDJI DOLMADAKIA

[Stuffed Grape Leaves (Meatless)]

This is a Greek version of a typical Near Eastern delicacy.

1 one-pound jar grape leaves
1 cup grated onion
¼ cup olive oil
2 teaspoons salt
1 cup rice
½ cup pignolia nuts (pine nuts)
½ cup dark raisins (optional)
1 teaspoon chopped parsley
½ teaspoon dill seed
1 teaspoon crushed mint
1 cup hot water
juice of 2 large lemons
4 cups warm water
¼ cup vegetable oil
1 lemon, sliced (for garnish)

Wash the grape leaves 3 times in cold water to remove brine. Then submerge them in boiling water and soak for 1 hour to soften.

To make the filling, heat the grated onion in a skillet to dry the moisture from it, then add the olive oil and simmer 5 minutes. Add 1 teaspoon of the salt, the rice, nuts, raisins, parsley, dill, mint, and hot water. Cover and simmer 10 minutes. The water should be completely absorbed. Stir in one half of the lemon juice and allow to cool.

In the bottom of a heavy kettle spread a layer of grape leaves. Separate the remaining leaves and remove the thick stem from each. Use 1 teaspoon to 1 tablespoon of filling for each leaf, depending on size dolmadakia desired. Place the filling at the end of the leaf, fold the sides of the leaf in over the filling and roll tightly with the shiny surface of the leaf on the outside. If stem end is on the outside, dolmadakia can be rolled tighter. Place them in layers in the kettle over the grape leaves. Pour over them the warm water, vegetable oil, and remaining lemon juice and salt. To keep them from unrolling while cooking, place a heavy plate over them inside the kettle. The water level will be above the plate. Cover the kettle and cook over a low flame for 25 minutes, at which time water should all be absorbed. Place on a platter to cool. Garnish with lemon slices and serve cold, each on a toothpick. Can be frozen or kept in refrigerator a week. *Makes about 50.*

RENGHA

[Smoked Herring]

1 large smoked herring
juice of 1 lemon
¼ cup olive oil

Place the fish on aluminum foil in the broiler pan. Set on lowest rack under broiler and heat, turning once, until the fish is hot through the center. Remove from broiler, cut off head and tail, split the back, and remove the bone. Cut the fish in small pieces and arrange on a serving plate. Beat together the lemon juice and olive oil and pour over the fish. Allow it to marinate ½ hour before serving. Serve on crackers.

This recipe can also be used for tsere, a small smoked Greek fish available in Greek stores. *Makes about 12 pieces.*

TYRI OREKTIKO

[Cheese Spread]

This is a pleasant blend of Greek and American flavors.

½ pound feta cheese, crumbled
½ pound cottage cheese (small curd, creamed)
1 eight-ounce package cream cheese
1 five-ounce jar blue cheese
2 tablespoons light cream
2 tablespoons muscatel wine
¼ teaspoon Worcestershire sauce
dash of nutmeg

Combine all ingredients in a bowl and beat with electric beater at medium speed until creamy. Place in jars and keep refrigerated until ready to use. Serve on crackers with an anchovy on top. *Makes 2½ pints spread for about 75 hors d'oeuvres.*

SERVED HOT

TARAMOKEFTEDES

[Tarama Balls]

1 cup tarama (1 eight-ounce jar Greek caviar)
2 cups mashed potatoes
2 small onions, finely grated
4 tablespoons chopped parsley

2 *tablespoons chopped mint*
1 *teaspoon dill seed*
¼ *teaspoon pepper*
½ *cup olive oil*
flour for coating
juice of 1 lemon

Combine tarama, potatoes, onions, parsley, mint, dill seed, pepper, and 1 tablespoon of the olive oil in a bowl and mix well. Shape into bite-size balls and roll in flour to coat. Heat the remaining olive oil in a skillet and fry the balls until golden brown. Place in a bowl and squeeze lemon juice over them. Serve warm on toothpicks.

This recipe can be used for large patties to be served as a main course during Lent. *Makes 36.*

MEEKRA KEFTEDAKIA

[Small Meat Balls with Sauce]

These can be served with or without sauce—usually plain for a cocktail snack and with sauce in a chafing dish for a buffet table.

MEAT BALLS:
1 *pound ground chuck beef*
1 *onion, minced*
2 *slices moistened bread, without crust*
1 *egg*
1 *teaspoon olive oil*
1 *tablespoon dry red wine*
1 *tablespoon tomato sauce*
¼ *teaspoon baking soda*
½ *teaspoon crushed mint*
1 *teaspoon salt*
¼ *teaspoon pepper*
flour for coating

vegetable oil (enough to deep-fry balls)
juice of 1 lemon (if not served with sauce)

SAUCE:
1 tablespoon flour
1 cup water
3 tablespoons fat from skillet
1 cup of tomato sauce
1 cup whole canned tomatoes
¼ cup dry red wine
juice of 1 lemon
1 tablespoon salt
dash of pepper
dash of sugar
serve with these.
1 teaspoon oregano

Combine all but last 3 ingredients for meat balls and mix well. Form into balls the size of a small walnut. Roll in flour and fry in the oil until brown and cooked through. Drain on paper towels. If sauce is to be made, save the fat from the skillet. If to be served without sauce, sprinkle lemon juice over them.

To make the sauce, blend the flour into water. Using the skillet in which the meat balls were cooked, retain 3 tablespoons of fat and blend in the flour and water mixture. Add remaining ingredients and cook, uncovered, stirring occasionally, 20 to 25 minutes until slightly thick. Add the meat balls to reheat, then transfer to a serving bowl or chafing dish. Serve hot with toothpicks. *Makes 36.*

TIGANITO TYRI

[Fried Cheese Squares]

In the tavernes of Athens these are served in a chafing dish or hot pan, often cooked right at the table. Hard, salty kefalotyri cheese does not melt. Retsina wine is the customary beverage to
½ teaspoon Tabasco sauce (or other hot pepper sauce)

1½ pounds kefalotyri cheese
¼ pound butter
juice of 1 lemon

Cut the cheese in 12 pieces. Heat the butter in a skillet or chafing dish. Add the cheese slices and fry until brown on both sides. Remove to a serving plate and cut slices into squares. Sprinkle with lemon juice and serve while hot. *Serves 12.*

TIGANITA SIKOTAKIA

[Fried Chicken Livers]

These are served in the tavernes with retsina wine.

1 pound chicken livers
½ cup olive oil
juice of 2 lemons
salt and pepper
oregano

Season the livers with salt, pepper, and oregano to taste. Heat the oil in a heavy skillet. When the oil is sizzling add the livers and fry on both sides until well done. Place on a platter and pour lemon juice over them. Cut in bite-size pieces and serve hot. *Serves 6 to 8.*

KALAMARAKIA

[Squid]

Miniature squid are used for hors d'oeuvres. This recipe can also be used for larger squid to be served as a fish dish.

1 pound squid, about 2 inches long
flour for coating
salt

½ cup olive oil
¼ cup sauterne wine
juice of 1 lemon

Wash the squid thoroughly and pull out the soft backbone and ink sac from head of each. Remove the black membrane from over whole squid. Coat them with flour and sprinkle with salt. Heat the olive oil in a heavy skillet and fry the squid until brown. Pour the wine over the squid, stir, and turn off the heat. Add lemon juice and stir. Let the squid stand in the sauce for 10 minutes, then drain. Arrange on a hot serving dish. Serve on small individual plates with forks. *Serves 12.*

GEARAKIA

[Fried Lamb Sundries]

This is popular with Greeks at outdoor gatherings. It is often cooked and served while a whole lamb is cooking on a spit.

The following from a young lamb:
  liver
  heart
  lung
salt and pepper
oregano
1 cup olive oil
juice of 3 lemons

Wash the liver, heart, and lung very well. Cut into 1-inch pieces and sprinkle with salt, pepper, and oregano to taste. In a heavy skillet heat the oil to sizzling. Add the organs and turn to brown on all sides. Lower the heat and continue cooking until cooked through. Place on a platter and pour the lemon juice over organs. Serve hot on toothpicks or on small individual plates with forks. *Serves 10 to 12.*

KOKORETSI

[Grilled Lamb Sundries]

This is usually cooked beside a whole lamb over an outdoor charcoal fire and is not recommended for indoor cooking. Some of the sundries are available only by special order.

The following from a young lamb:
  heart
  liver
  sweetbread
  lung
  intestine
  lamb casing (membrane from the side of the large intestine)
salt and pepper
1 tablespoon oregano
juice of 3 lemons
1 cup olive oil

Wash all the organs 3 or 4 times. Salt the intestine well, then using a pencil or stick to force end of intestine through center, turn it inside out. Wash it again 3 or 4 times. Drain organs well and cut all but casing and intestine in pieces just large enough to be held on a long spit. Arrange them alternately on the spit and sprinkle with salt and pepper.

Combine the oregano, lemon juice, and olive oil, and brush over entire surface. Wrap the casing around the meat. Twine the intestine around, knotting it to make very secure on the spit. Brush again with oil and lemon juice. Set aside for 1 hour to absorb seasoning, then place spit over a slow-burning charcoal fire and cook 3 hours, basting occasionally with remaining oil and lemon juice. If spit is not motorized, turn it every 20 minutes. Cut in small pieces to serve. *Serves 10 to 12.*

TYROPITAKIA

[Cheese-filled Triangles]

These are especially popular for the five o'clock social hour. Read the directions for handling fillo on page 176 before beginning recipe.

¾ pound feta cheese
4 ounces cottage cheese (large curd, creamed)
1 egg plus 2 yolks
1 tablespoon light cream
dash of nutmeg
1 pound fillo
1 pound butter, melted

In a bowl blend together the feta cheese and cottage cheese. Add the eggs, cream, and nutmeg and blend well. Cut the fillo into strips 3 inches wide. Brush with melted butter. Place a teaspoon of filling in center 1 inch from end. Fold one corner over in a triangle. Fold in the edges about ⅛ inch, then continue turning over the triangle to end of fillo strip, buttering it well with each turn. Place triangles on a cookie sheet, brush tops with butter, and bake at 325 degrees for 35 minutes or until brown. Remove from pan immediately and serve hot. *Makes about 60.*

SPANAKOPITAKIA

[Spinach-filled Triangles]

This is another cocktail-time favorite. Read the directions for handling fillo on page 176 and also those for wrapping triangles as in Tyropitakia.

1 pound fresh spinach or 2 packages frozen chopped
1 small onion, grated

2 tablespoons butter
2 eggs plus 4 yolks, slightly beaten
½ pound feta cheese
½ teaspoon salt
½ teaspoon nutmeg
1 teaspoon chopped parsley
1 tablespoon grated toast
½ pound fillo
½ pound butter, melted

If using fresh spinach, steam it until wilted, then chop. For frozen spinach, defrost completely and drain well. Sauté the onion in the 2 tablespoons butter. Add the spinach and cook until dry. Remove from heat and add eggs, cheese, salt, nutmeg, parsley, and grated toast, mixing well. Cool before proceeding as for Tyropitakia. Bake at 325 degrees for 35 minutes. Remove from pan immediately and serve hot. *Makes about 30.*

KREATOPITAKIA

[Meat-filled Triangles]

This version of triangles is also served in late afternoon. Read directions for handling fillo on page 176 and for wrapping triangles as in Tyropitakia.

1 small onion, finely chopped
1 tablespoon olive oil
¾ pound lean ground chuck beef
¼ pound lean ground pork
¼ cup dry red wine
2 tablespoons tomato sauce
¼ cup water
1 egg, slightly beaten

½ cup grated kefalotyri cheese (or Parmesan or Romano)
2 tablespoons grated toast
1 pound fillo
1 pound butter, melted

Sauté the onion in the oil, add the meat, and brown well. Drain off any fat. Combine the liquids and add to the meat. Cover and simmer 30 minutes. Remove from heat, add egg, cheese, and grated toast and blend well. Cool the sauce, then proceed to make triangles as in Tyropitakia. Bake at 325 degrees for 35 minutes. Remove from pan immediately and serve hot. *Makes about 60.*

HIRINO KRASSATO

[Pork Cooked in Wine]

This is served both at cocktail time and to late-evening patrons in the tavernes.

2½ pounds pork butt
salt and pepper
1 teaspoon oregano
1 tablespoon vegetable oil
2 cups dry red wine
juice of 1 lemon

Cut fat away from meat, then cut into 1-inch cubes. Sprinkle with salt, pepper, and oregano. Heat the oil in a skillet and brown the meat well. Drain off the fat, then add the wine, cover, and simmer for 1 hour. Add the lemon juice, toss to coat meat cubes evenly, and cook 5 minutes longer. Serve hot from a chafing dish with toothpicks. *Serves 30.*

SOUPS

ZOUMOS *[Concentrated Meat or Chicken Stock]*

ZOUMOS ME THIOSMO *[Lamb or Beef Broth with Mint]*

TRAHANA SOUPA *[Pasta Soup]*

FIDÉ SOUPA *[Fidelini Soup]*

AVGOLEMONO SOUPA *[Egg and Lemon Soup]*

MAYIRITSA *[Easter Soup]*

FAKI *[Lentil Soup]*

FASOULADA *[Bean Soup]*

HORTO SOUPA *[Thick Vegetable Soup]*

PSAROSOUPA *[Fish Soup]*

KAKAVIA *[Fresh Sardine Soup]*

5 · Soups

BECAUSE SOUPS are nourishing, easy to prepare, and economical, they are prepared frequently by Greek cooks. Everyday soups are often creative concoctions of left-overs with some fresh vegetables and herbs added to spruce up the flavor, but more exact methods are followed to make the soups for special holidays and formal occasions.

The base of many good Greek soups is meat or chicken stock. Greeks most often use the more plentiful lamb, but Americans generally prefer beef. Concentrated stock can be made in quantity, frozen in ice cube trays, and stored in plastic containers in the freezer to be thawed in any quantity when needed.

ZOUMOS

[Concentrated Meat or Chicken Stock]

4 pounds lean meat and bones of beef, lamb, or chicken
1 onion, chopped

1 *stalk celery, chopped*
1 *tablespoon salt*
2 *quarts water*

Combine all ingredients in a large kettle. Cover and simmer 2 to 3 hours. Strain into a large bowl and cool. (Pieces of meat can be saved to use in soup or as a side dish with soup.) Remove the fat from top of cool stock. Heat stock enough to liquify and pour into ice cube trays to freeze for storage. When using stock it can be diluted with an equal quantity of water. *Yields 1½ quarts of stock.*

ZOUMOS ME THIOSMO

[Lamb or Beef Broth with Mint]

This is served in summer. It is also a good soup for invalids.

3 *cups lamb or beef stock*
4 *sprigs fresh mint*
4 *wedges lemon*

Heat the stock to boiling and drop in the mint sprigs a few seconds before serving. Include a sprig in each bowlful and serve a lemon wedge on the side. *Serves 4.*

TRAHANA SOUPA

[Pasta Soup]

Trahana is a homemade pasta meal which is an important staple of Greek villagers. This makes a very filling and nourishing soup.

3 *cups meat stock*
1½ *cups canned tomatoes*
1 *teaspoon salt*

¾ cup Trahana (page 242)
croutons (for garnish)

Combine the meat stock and tomatoes in a saucepan and boil gently 10 minutes. Add the salt, then very gradually add the Trahana, stirring constantly to avoid forming lumps. Continue boiling gently, uncovered, for 20 minutes. This is a thick soup but it can be made thinner by using more meat stock. Serve with croutons. *Serves 4.*

FIDÉ SOUPA

[Fidelini Soup]

Fidelini is a noodle product so fine it resembles shredded wheat. It is also packaged under the names "Fideos," or as "Fine Noodles in Nests."

4 cups meat or chicken stock
1 cup canned tomatoes
1 teaspoon salt
4 rolls fidelini, crushed
¼ cup grated kefalotyri cheese (or Parmesan or Romano)

Combine stock and tomatoes in a saucepan, cover and boil gently 10 minutes. Add salt and crushed fidelini and continue boiling gently, uncovered, for 10 minutes. Sprinkle grated cheese over each bowlful. *Serves 4.*

Variations: Substitute ½ cup Hilopites (Greek Noodles, page 241), orzo, or rice for the fidelini and cook 18 to 20 minutes.

AVGOLEMONO SOUPA

[Egg and Lemon Soup]

This is the best known and most elegant of the Greek soups. It is served with dinner, especially for formal occasions. We

think it best with chicken stock and rice, but it can be varied
as noted.

> 6 *cups chicken stock*
> *salt*
> ½ *cup rice*
> 1 *teaspoon flour*
> ¼ *cup water*
> 3 *eggs*
> *juice of 2 lemons*

Bring the stock to a boil and add salt and rice. Cover and boil
gently 18 minutes. Measure out 3 cups of the stock into a small
saucepan. Cover the remaining stock and rice and keep hot.
Make a paste of the flour and water, add to the 3 cups of stock
and boil gently for 5 minutes. In a large bowl beat the eggs with
electric beater until very thick and light in color. Add, by the
spoonful, the boiling stock and lemon juice alternately while continuing to beat. Continue beating a few minutes after all is added,
then stir into hot rice soup, blending thoroughly. Do not cover
or return to fire or it will curdle. Serve immediately. *Serves 6.*

Variations: Lamb, veal, or beef stock can be substituted for
the chicken stock. In place of rice, ½ cup of orzo or Hilopites
(Greek Noodles, page 241) can be used and cooked 18 to 20
minutes. Four rolls of fidelini can also be substituted for rice and
cooked 10 minutes.

MAYIRITSA

[Easter Soup]

This is the famous soup made from the entrails of the paschal
lamb and served at the home meal following midnight Easter
Eve church services.

The following from a young lamb:
  liver
  heart
  lung
1 lamb intestine
¼ pound butter
1 onion, chopped
hot lamb stock or water to cover
1 tablespoon salt
1 teaspoon pepper
4 bunches scallions, chopped
1 tablespoon fresh chopped dill
  (or 1 teaspoon dry)
⅓ cup rice
1 teaspoon flour
¼ cup water
3 eggs
juice of 2 lemons

Wash the meat organs 3 or 4 times. Salt the intestine well, turn inside out using a pencil to force the end through the inside. Wash the intestine well again. Place the organs in a large kettle, cover with water, and heat to scalding. Drain and wash again in hot water. Spread on a bread board and cut the organs into 1-inch pieces. In a large heavy kettle melt the butter and sauté the onion. Add the meat and sauté a few minutes, then add the hot stock or water and salt and pepper. Cover and cook slowly about 3 hours or until all the meat is very tender. Add the scallions and dill and cook another 10 minutes. Measure the stock and add water, if necessary, to make 3 cups. Bring to a boil, add the rice, cover, and cook 20 minutes longer.

Transfer 1 cup of stock from the soup to a small saucepan. Blend the flour and the ¼ cup cold water into a paste, add to stock, and heat to boiling. Beat the eggs until very thick. Continue to beat while adding, alternately, the hot stock and lemon juice. Add to the hot soup and blend thoroughly. Do not cover or reheat. Serve immediately. *Serves 6.*

FAKI

[Lentil Soup]

This or the following bean soup is the only food eaten by devout Orthodox Greeks on Good Friday. The vinegar seasoning is symbolic, recalling that it was given to Christ on the Cross.

1 cup dry lentils
10 cups water
1 tablespoon salt
¼ teaspoon pepper
1 stalk celery, diced
1 onion, chopped
1 clove garlic, chopped
wine vinegar (for seasoning)

Put the lentils in a large kettle with 4 cups of the water and 1 teaspoon of the salt. Bring to a boil, then pour out the water and drain. Combine the lentils in the kettle with all the other ingredients except the vinegar, cover, and simmer 1½ to 2 hours. Serve with a little vinegar on top of each bowl. *Serves 4.*

FASOULADA

[Bean Soup]

This meatless soup can be made with dried navy beans, lima beans, or chick peas. It is a main dish for a family meal or can be used as Good Friday soup made from navy beans with the olive oil omitted.

1 pound dry beans
2 onions
2 stalks celery
3 carrots
2 cups canned tomatoes
⅓ cup olive oil (omit for Good Friday)
3 quarts water
1 tablespoon salt
½ teaspoon pepper
wine vinegar (for seasoning)

Wash the beans and soak overnight in cold water. Drain. Cut the onion, celery, and carrots into small pieces and combine with drained beans in a large kettle. Add tomatoes, olive oil, water, salt, and pepper. Cover and simmer at least 4 hours. Serve with a little vinegar on top of each bowl. *Serves 8 to 10.*

HORTO SOUPA

[Thick Vegetable Soup]

If this is a Lenten soup omit the stock and butter and add 3 tablespoons olive oil.

2 large onions
1 small head celery
5 carrots
4 small zucchini (about ½ pound)
3 leeks
½ cup fresh lima beans or soaked dried beans
3 fresh ripe tomatoes
1 tablespoon salt
1½ quarts water (or enough to cover vegetables)
1 cup meat stock
1 tablespoon butter
croutons (for garnish)

Wash the vegetables, cut into medium-size pieces, and put in a large kettle. Add salt, cover with water, and cook, covered, for 1½ hours. Remove the vegetables from liquid and purée them in an electric blender or by forcing through a colander. Return the purée to the liquid in the kettle. Add the stock and butter, cover, and cook 15 minutes longer. Serve with croutons on top. *Serves 6 to 8.*

PSAROSOUPA

[Fish Soup]

Many Greek islanders and coastal people use this hearty soup as a main course. It is served frequently during Lent and on other meatless days.

2 pounds fresh cod or other white fish or mixed shellfish
juice of 1 lemon
2½ teaspoons salt
¾ teaspoon pepper
2 large onions, sliced
1 cup diced celery
1 cup diced carrots
1 cup canned tomatoes
¼ cup chopped parsley
3 bay leaves
½ cup olive oil
4 cups water
croutons (for garnish)

Wash the fish, sprinkle with lemon juice, ½ teaspoon of the salt, and ¼ teaspoon of the pepper, and set aside. Combine all other ingredients in a large saucepan, cover, and simmer 25 minutes. Add the fish and cook, covered, 10 minutes. Remove the fish and pick out the bones. Return the fish to the soup, cover, and cook 15 minutes longer. Serve with croutons on top. *Serves 6 to 8.*

KAKAVIA

[Fresh Sardine Soup]

This recipe originated in Filiates, a village of northwest Greece, inland a few miles from the coast looking toward Corfu. It takes its name from the antique utensil in which it is cooked, a copper kettle which fits into a tripod over an open fire. These kettles are still in use today in a few remote villages.

2 large onions, chopped
2 cups canned tomatoes
½ cup olive oil
salt and pepper
2 quarts water
2 pounds tiny fresh sardines
croutons (for garnish)

Combine all ingredients except sardines in a kettle, cover, and cook 30 minutes. Wash the fish, drop into the hot soup, and cook 20 minutes or until fish have cooked to a pulp. Strain in a colander, forcing the pulp through. Return to stove and cook 5 minutes longer. Serve with croutons on top. *Serves 6 to 8.*

SALADS

HORTA VRASTA SALATA *[Cold Boiled Vegetables for Salad]*
OMMA HORTARIKA SALATA *[Fresh Raw Vegetables for Salad]*
SALATA MAROULI *[Lettuce Salad]*
SALATA *[Greek Salad]*
PANTZARIA SALATA *[Beet Salad]*
PATATOSALATA *[Potato Salad]*
MELIDZANO SALATA *[Eggplant Salad]*
DOMATES YEMISTES ME GARIDES SALATA *[Tomato Stuffed with Shrimp Salad]*
TARAMOSALATA *[Caviar Salad]*
PORTOCALE-YAOURTE SALATA *[Orange-Yogurt Salad Mold]*

6 · Salads

THE ART of salad making comes naturally to the Greeks, who have an abundant and varied assortment of greens and other vegetables available most of the year, often from the family garden.

Salads are assembled in artistic arrangements on individual plates rather than being served from a bowl as a tossed salad. Black olives, pieces of Feta cheese, anchovy fillets, and tomato wedges are often used in a leafy salad or to garnish salad platters for buffet tables.

Olive oil and wine vinegar seasoned with oregano is the standard dressing for leafy greens. Lemon juice is sometimes a substitute for wine vinegar, especially if the salad contains seafood.

Greeks do not generally use fruits in salad, preferring instead to serve fresh fruit at the end of the meal. The Orange-Yogurt Salad Mold recipe given in this chapter was developed in a Greek homemaking school where methods are sought for wider use of the most abundant foods. This departure from tradition is one illustration of the evolutionary process at work in Greek cookery today.

HORTA VRASTA SALATA

[Cold Boiled Vegetables for Salad]

The Greeks often serve boiled asparagus, cauliflower, green beans, peas, or zucchini cold as a salad. Vegetables should be boiled until just tender but still firm. Mix together and pour over them before serving:

¼ cup olive oil
juice of 1 lemon
salt and pepper

OMMA HORTARIKA SALATA

[Fresh Raw Vegetables for Salad]

The following are served with the same oil-and-lemon-juice dressing as for Cold Boiled Vegetables: sliced cucumbers (with a pinch of oregano); tomato and sweet onion slices (always with oregano); tomato and green pepper slices; grated carrots (with chopped parsley); tender dandelion greens; endive.

SALATA MAROULI

[Lettuce Salad]

2 very small heads lettuce
12 Kalamata olives
⅓ cup olive oil
¼ cup wine vinegar
½ teaspoon salt
1 teaspoon oregano

Wash lettuce, remove best outer leaves, and arrange on 4 individual plates. Cut lettuce heads in quarters and put 2 sections on each plate. Place 3 olives around edge of each plate. Combine olive oil, vinegar, salt, and oregano and pour over salads. *Serves 4.*

SALATA

[Greek Salad]

1 *small head lettuce*
1 *small cucumber, thinly sliced*
1 *small bunch radishes, sliced*
3 *scallions, cut in short pieces*
2 *firm red tomatoes, cut in wedges*
12 *Kalamata olives*
⅓ *cup olive oil*
¼ *cup wine vinegar*
1 *teaspoon salt*
1 *teaspoon oregano*
4 *slices feta cheese*
8 *anchovy fillets*

In a large bowl shred the lettuce and add cucumber, radishes, scallions, tomatoes, and olives. Mix together the olive oil, vinegar, salt, and oregano and pour over the vegetables. Toss to mix well, then serve into 4 individual bowls. Place a slice of cheese and 2 anchovy fillets over top of each. *Serves 4.*

PANTZARIA SALATA

[Beet Salad]

1 *bunch fresh beets with tops*
1 *clove garlic, minced*
salt and pepper
¼ *cup olive oil*
3 *tablespoons wine vinegar*

Cut off beet tops, scrub beets, and boil beets in their skins until tender. Clean leaves and stems, cut stems in short pieces, and add to beet water to cook until tender. Cool and peel the beets, cut in slices, and place in a bowl with drained stems and leaves. Add the minced garlic, salt, and pepper. Combine olive oil and vinegar and pour over beets. Place in refrigerator for several hours before serving. *Serves 4.*

Variation: Skordalia (Garlic Sauce), pages 238, 239, can be substituted for the olive oil and vinegar.

PATATOSALATA

[Potato Salad]

1 pound white potatoes
1 small sweet onion, grated
1 tablespoon fresh finely chopped parsley or 1 teaspoon oregano
12 Kalamata olives
2 hardboiled eggs, diced (omit during Lent)
¼ cup olive oil
juice of 1 lemon or 3 tablespoons wine vinegar
salt and pepper

Boil the potatoes in their skins until cooked through. Cool, peel, and cut in small cubes. Combine them in a bowl with onion, parsley or oregano, olives, and hardboiled eggs. Mix together the olive oil, lemon juice or vinegar, salt, and pepper and pour over the salad. Toss to mix well and place in refrigerator for several hours before serving. *Serves 4.*

MELIDZANO SALATA

[Eggplant Salad]

The eggplant is handled in a special way in this recipe to retain good color and make it easy to seed. Avoid discoloration by using only stainless-steel or wooden utensils.

2 pounds small eggplants
1 cup water
salt
½ small onion, grated
1 tablespoon chopped parsley
⅓ cup olive oil
3 tablespoons wine vinegar
dash of pepper
6 lettuce leaves
3 medium-size firm fresh tomatoes
12 Kalamata olives

Wash eggplants and place whole and unpeeled in a saucepan
with 1 cup water. Cover and steam until cooked through. They
will become shriveled. Pour off water, run cold water into the
kettle and let stand 10 minutes. Drain, peel off skin, cut in half,
and remove seeds, using a stainless-steel knife. Sprinkle with salt
and place in a stainless-steel colander or cheesecloth bag to
drain well. Turn into a wooden bowl and mash with a wooden
spoon. Add onion, parsley, olive oil, vinegar, and pepper and mix
well. Chill well before serving. To serve, place a scoop of eggplant salad on a lettuce leaf and surround with tomato wedges
and Kalamata olives. *Serves 6.*

DOMATES YEMISTES ME GARIDES SALATA

[Tomato Stuffed with Shrimp Salad]

1 pound small boiled shrimp (page 87)
1 tablespoon grated onion
8 Kalamata olives, pitted and cut into small pieces
½ cup olive oil
juice of 1 lemon
1 teaspoon salt

½ *teaspoon oregano*
4 large firm tomatoes, chilled
4 lettuce leaves

Clean shrimp and cut into small pieces. In a bowl combine with onion, olives, oil, lemon, salt, and oregano. Mix together well. Cut across tops and scoop out centers of tomatoes. Place each on a lettuce leaf on a plate. Stuff the tomatoes with shrimp mixture. *Serves 4.*

Variation: Using the same combination of ingredients, mound the shrimp mixture on lettuce leaves and surround with tomato wedges.

TARAMOSALATA

[Caviar Salad]

Tarama is a popular delicacy available in glass jars in importing shops. This recipe can be used for an hors d'oeuvre spread as well as for salad.

1 eight-ounce jar tarama (Greek caviar)
1 small boiled potato, mashed
1 slice bread without crust, moistened
juice of 2 lemons
1 cup olive oil
½ small onion, grated (optional)
8 lettuce leaves
chopped parsley (for garnish)
8 Kalamata olives (for garnish)

Combine all ingredients except parsley and olives in a mixing bowl. Beat with electric beater until smooth. Place scoops on individual lettuce leaves. Sprinkle a little chopped parsley over top and press an olive in center. *Serves 8.*

PORTOCALE-YAOURTE SALATA

[Orange-Yogurt Salad Mold]

2 *cups orange juice*
½ *cup sugar*
3 *envelopes unflavored gelatin*
½ *cup water*
1 *pint yogurt*

Combine orange juice and sugar in a saucepan, heat to boiling, and stir until sugar dissolves. Soften the gelatin in water, add to boiling orange juice, and stir until thoroughly dissolved. Allow to cool. Put the yogurt in a bowl, add a few tablespoons of the cooled liquid, and beat to blend well. Add balance of juice and blend. Pour into an oiled 1-quart ring mold and put in refrigerator to set at least 5 hours. To serve, turn the mold out on a bed of lettuce on a serving plate. Fill the center with fresh or canned fruit that has been well drained. *Serves 8.*

VEGETABLES

LAHANIKA VRASTA [Boiled or Steamed Vegetables]

LAHANIKA YAHNI ME DOMATES [Sautéed Vegetables in Tomato Sauce]

PANTZARIA SKORDALIA [Beets with Garlic Sauce]

PATATES PSITES [Baked Potatoes]

PATATES POUTENKA [Potato Pudding]

LAHANIKA STO FOURNO [Vegetables in Casserole]

ANGINARES POLITIKES [Stewed Vegetables with Artichokes]

LAHANO PATATES KAI DOMATES [Cabbage and Potatoes with Tomato Sauce]

KOUNOUPIDI-KOLOKITHAKIA ME DOMATES [Cauliflower or Zucchini with Tomato Sauce]

MELIDZANES TIGANITES-KOLOKITHAKIA SKORDALIA [Fried Eggplant or Zucchini with Garlic Sauce]

SPANAKORIZO [Spinach and Rice]

BIZELIA, PASTA KAI DOMATES [Peas, and Tomatoes with Macaroni]

7 · Vegetables

GREEKS HAVE a flair for vegetable cookery—a compensation for their many meatless days. Almost every vegetable known to us also grows in Greece, and there are a number of wild greens and herbs to use as well.

The Greeks are especially fond of dandelion greens. A springtime traveler to Greece will see housewives scattered over the hillsides filling baskets with fresh wild greens. The dandelions are good only in the spring when they are mild flavored and very tender.

Vegetables are often cooked in combination dishes with meat, rice, or pasta, but when cooked alone they are usually prepared in one of two ways: they are either boiled and served with olive oil and lemon juice over them, or sautéed and then cooked in a tomato sauce. Tomatoes and onions are used generously in Greek cookery but are never cooked alone as a dish in themselves.

Some vegetables require preliminary preparation to insure good flavor, texture, or color. Artichokes, eggplant, and okra should be treated according to the following directions:

Artichokes—The fresh artichokes shipped to our midwestern and eastern markets are usually too large and fibrous to be suitable for Greek dishes. If very small fresh ones are not available, use frozen or canned hearts. To treat fresh artichokes, wash them thoroughly, cut off tough outer leaves and leaf ends at top. Cut them in half and remove the prickly choke, including fiber inside heart. Thoroughly coat them with lemon juice and let stand for 30 minutes. Frozen hearts should be placed in a bowl and thoroughly covered with lemon juice to stand while defrosting. Drain canned hearts and cover with lemon juice to stand 15 minutes. The lemon juice prevents discoloration.

Eggplant—Peel off the purple skin and slice lengthwise in ½-inch-thick slices unless to be used whole. Salt each slice very heavily on both sides and place in a bowl to stand for 30 minutes. Pour cold water over the eggplant and let stand 10 minutes longer. Squeeze the water out and blot dry with paper towels. The natural bitterness will be gone.

Okra—It is desirable to remove the gelatinous matter from okra before cooking. Wash, cut off the stems, and place okra in a bowl. Pour strong vinegar over it, using ½ cup per pound of okra. Let it stand 1 hour, then wash thoroughly with cold water. Frozen okra should be dropped in boiling water to defrost. When pieces have separated, pour off the water, drain well, and place in a bowl. Add ½ cup vinegar and let stand 15 minutes. Wash thoroughly in hot water and drain. Drain canned okra and treat with vinegar the same way.

The most usual ways of cooking vegetables Greek style and the particular vegetables suitable for each method are described below.

LAHANIKA VRASTA
[Boiled or Steamed Vegetables]

This method is suitable for:

| all leafy greens | asparagus | cabbage |
| artichokes | beets | carrots |

| cauliflower | green beans | potatoes |
| endive | peas | zucchini |

Approximately 1 pound fresh vegetables
water
1 very small onion, chopped
1 teaspoon salt
¼ cup olive oil
juice of 1 lemon

Wash and prepare vegetables and put in a saucepan with as little water as is necessary to keep them from burning during cooking. Add onion and salt, cover and cook until just tender. Drain and serve with oil and lemon juice poured over top. *Serves 4.*

LAHANIKA YAHNI ME DOMATES

[Sautéed Vegetables in Tomato Sauce]

This method is suitable for:

artichokes	green beans	*potatoes
cabbage	leeks	spinach
*cauliflower	*okra	*zucchini
*cggplant	peas	

The vegetables marked * should be fried before using, the others can be just lightly sautéed. See directions, pages 61–62 for first treating artichokes, eggplant, and okra.

Carrots can be combined in the sauté with cauliflower, green beans, potatoes, or peas. Try seasoning cauliflower and potatoes with cinnamon, and use parsley with eggplant, potatoes, and zucchini.

Approximately 1 pound fresh vegetables
⅓ cup olive oil
1 onion, chopped

½ to 1 cup hot water
1 teaspoon salt
¼ teaspoon pepper
1 tablespoon flour
¼ cup cold water
1½ cups canned tomatoes

Wash and prepare vegetables. Be sure they are well drained. Heat the oil in a heavy saucepan, add the onion and vegetable, and sauté until very light brown. Add hot water, salt, and pepper, cover, and simmer 10 to 15 minutes or until vegetables are cooked through but still firm. Make a paste of the flour and water, and combine with tomatoes in a saucepan. Heat to boiling and add to vegetables. Continue cooking 10 to 15 minutes. *Serves 4.*

PANTZARIA SKORDALIA

[Beets with Garlic Sauce]

2 bunches small beets with tops
1 small onion, chopped
1½ cups water
1½ teaspoons salt
Skordalia (Garlic Sauce), pages 238, 239

Peel the beets and cut in quarters. Chop the tender stems and leaves. Combine beets and tops with chopped onion in a saucepan. Add water and salt, cover, and boil gently until beets are done. Drain well. Have Skordalia ready and spread over beets before serving. *Serves 4.*

PATATES PSITES

[Baked Potatoes]

4 large baking potatoes
¼ cup feta cheese

4 tablespoons butter
2 teaspoons salt
¼ teaspoon pepper
dash of nutmeg
2 tablespoons grated kefalotyri cheese (or Parmesan or
Romano)

Scrub the potatoes, rub skins with oil, and bake in 400-degree
oven for 1 hour. Slash tops, scoop out potato and place in a bowl.
Mash well, then add feta cheese, butter, salt, pepper, and nutmeg.
Mix well and stuff in potato skins. Sprinkle grated cheese over
tops and return to hot oven for 5 to 10 minutes to brown. *Serves 4.*

PATATES POUTENKA

[Potato Pudding]

This is a good entrée accompaniment for a formal dinner.

1 pound white potatoes
2 tablespoons farina
3 eggs
1 teaspoon salt
¼ teaspoon nutmeg
1¼ cups warm milk
¼ cup grated kefalotyri cheese plus ¼ cup for topping (or
Parmesan or Romano)

Boil potatoes in their skins until cooked through. Cool, peel,
and mash in a bowl. Add other ingredients and beat with electric
beater until smooth. Spread in a buttered 8x8x2-inch casserole or
Pyrex baking dish. Sprinkle ¼ cup grated cheese on top. Bake
at 350 degrees 20 minutes or until top is brown. *Serves 6.*

LAHANIKA STO FOURNO

[Vegetables in Casserole]

This is a typical main course for Small Lent, August 1 to 15, when all vegetables are plentiful. American cooks will find it an ideal accompaniment for meat on a buffet supper table. If this is not a Lenten dish 1 cup meat stock and 3 tablespoons butter dotted over vegetables can be substituted for olive oil.

4 very small eggplants, cut in halves
½ pound okra
8 very small zucchini
12 tiny whole potatoes (or pieces walnut size)
12 small white onions
6 small carrots, cut in half crosswise
4 small green peppers, cut in half
½ pound green beans, in 3-inch lengths
2 stalks celery, in 1-inch pieces
1 tablespoon salt
½ teaspoon pepper
½ teaspoon dill seed
½ cup finely chopped parsley
1 cup olive oil
1 cup water
½ cup dry white wine
8 medium-size fresh ripe tomatoes
1 tablespoon flour
¼ cup water
½ cup grated kefalotyri cheese (or Parmesan or Romano, omit for Lent)

Use a very large casserole or Pyrex pan about 13x11x3 inches. Treat eggplants and okra according to directions on page 62. Wash and pare vegetables and arrange in casserole. Sprinkle salt, pepper, dill, and parsley over them. Pour the olive oil, water, and wine over vegetables, distributing evenly. Cover the casserole tightly with its own lid or aluminum foil and bake at 325 degrees for 30 minutes.

In a saucepan mash the tomatoes. Make a paste of flour and water, add to tomatoes, and cook until slightly thick. Pour over the vegetables. Replace cover and continue baking 30 minutes or until all are done. Sprinkle cheese on top, if desired, and put under broiler 5 minutes to brown. *Serves 8 to 10 as main entree or 12 to 15 as meat accompaniment.*

ANGINARES POLITIKES

[Stewed Vegetables with Artichokes]

2 packages frozen artichoke hearts
12 small whole white onions
12 small whole potatoes (or pieces walnut size)
6 small carrots cut in half crosswise
3 stalks celery, in 2-inch pieces
2 cups water
1 tablespoon flour
½ cup olive or vegetable oil
juice of 1 lemon
2 teaspoons salt
½ teaspoon pepper
½ teaspoon dill seed

Follow directions for treating artichokes on pages 61–62. Pare the other vegetables. With a little of the water make a paste of the flour, then combine water, flour paste, oil, lemon juice, and seasonings in a large heavy kettle. Cook about 10 minutes, stirring to keep liquid smooth as it thickens. Add the vegetables, except artichokes, cover, and simmer 30 minutes. Add the artichokes, shaking the pan to cover them with sauce. Cover and cook 15 minutes longer. Carefully transfer the vegetables to a serving bowl so that they do not break into pieces. *Serves 10 to 12.*

LAHANO PATATES KAI DOMATES

[Cabbage and Potatoes with Tomato Sauce]

This is an inexpensive but filling dish, ideal for large families.

4 medium-size potatoes
2 tablespoons lemon juice
1½ teaspoons salt
⅓ teaspoon pepper
1 two-pound head of cabbage
⅓ cup olive oil
1 large onion, thinly sliced
1 cup hot water
3 tablespoons vegetable oil
2 cups canned tomatoes
1 tablespoon flour
¼ cup cold water

Peel and cut the potatoes in quarters. Put them in a bowl and sprinkle with lemon juice, ½ teaspoon of the salt, and a little of the pepper. Wash and core the cabbage and cut in 6 pieces. In a large heavy saucepan heat the olive oil, add onion and cabbage, and sauté about 10 minutes. Add the remaining salt, pepper and the hot water. Cover and cook until cabbage is soft but not fully cooked. Heat the vegetable oil in a skillet and fry the potatoes until brown. Add to the cabbage and cook together 10 minutes. Remove all but 1 tablespoon oil from the skillet, make a paste of the flour and water, add flour paste and tomatoes to skillet, and bring to a boil. Add the mixture to cabbage and potatoes and cook 15 minutes longer. *Serves 6.*

KOUNOUPIDI-KOLOKITHAKIA ME DOMATES

[Cauliflower or Zucchini with Tomato Sauce]

1 large head cauliflower
or 12 very small whole zucchini
salt and pepper
cinnamon (omit with zucchini)
⅓ cup olive or vegetable oil (more if necessary)
1 medium-size onion, chopped
4 small carrots, cut crosswise
1¼ cups water
1 tablespoon flour
1½ cups canned tomatoes
juice of ½ lemon
½ cup grated kefalotyri cheese (or Parmesan or Romano, optional)

Core the cauliflower and cut it in about 8 pieces. If using zucchini, leave very small ones whole or use fewer larger ones cut in pieces. Sprinkle with salt, pepper, and cinnamon (the last for cauliflower only). In a heavy kettle or Dutch oven heat the oil and fry the cauliflower or zucchini until brown, then remove to a bowl. Sauté the onion and carrots, then return the other fried vegetables to the kettle. Add 1 cup of water, cover, and cook 5 minutes if zucchini or 15 minutes if cauliflower. Make a paste of the flour and remaining ¼ cup of the water. In a small saucepan combine tomatoes, flour paste, lemon juice, another teaspoon of salt, dash of pepper, and dash of cinnamon (for cauliflower). Bring to a boil, then add to vegetables and cook 15 minutes or until vegetables are done. Sprinkle cheese over top before serving, if desired, except if a Lenten dish. *Serves 6 to 8.*

MELIDZANES TIGANITES-KOLOKITHAKIA SKORDALIA

[Fried Eggplant or Zucchini with Garlic Sauce]

2 medium-size eggplants or 4 large zucchini
1 egg
1 tablespoon milk
3 tablespoons flour
1 teaspoon salt
1 cup olive or vegetable oil
½ cup Skordalia (Garlic Sauce), pages 238, 239

Cut the vegetables in slices ½ to 1 inch thick. If using egg-plant, treat first according to directions on page 62. Blend the egg, milk, flour, and salt into a batter. Heat half the oil in a skillet. Coat the vegetable slices with batter and fry until brown on both sides and cooked through center. Add more oil to skillet as needed. After slices are fried, drain on paper towels and arrange on a plate. Spread the Skordalia over top. *Serves 4 to 6.*

Variation: For Lent, substitute cracker crumbs for the batter. Use Lenten Skordalia (page 239) or sprinkle juice of 1 lemon over fried vegetables.

SPANAKORIZO

[Spinach and Rice]

This is a good Lenten dish. We recommend making it only with fresh spinach.

1 pound fresh spinach
⅓ cup olive oil
1 onion, chopped

1 bunch small scallions with tops, chopped
1½ cups hot water
2 fresh ripe tomatoes
2 tablespoons tomato sauce
2 teaspoons salt
dash of pepper
½ cup rice

Wash the spinach well and remove any tough stems. Set aside to drain thoroughly. Heat the oil in a saucepan, add the onions and scallions, and sauté until light brown. Add the water, tomatoes, tomato sauce, salt, pepper and rice, cover, and cook for 15 minutes. Add the spinach, toss with a fork to mix well, cover, and cook 5 to 10 minutes longer. *Serves 6.*

Variation: Fresh leeks (prasa) can be substituted for spinach in the above recipe but require longer cooking. This is a famous dish of Argos in the eastern Peloponnesus where leeks grow in abundance.

BIZELIA, PASTA KAI DOMATES

[Peas, and Tomatoes with Macaroni]

This makes a good Lenten dish.

¼ cup vegetable oil
1 medium-size onion, chopped
1½ cups canned tomatoes
2 teaspoons salt
¼ teaspoon pepper
1 cup hot water
¾ cup small shell-shape macaroni
2 cups cooked or canned peas

Heat oil in a saucepan and sauté onion. Add the tomatoes, salt, and pepper, cover, and cook 10 minutes. Add water and bring to a boil. Add macaroni, cover, and cook 10 minutes. Drain the peas, add, and cook 10 minutes longer. *Serves 4.*

FISH AND SEAFOOD

PSARI TIS SKARAS *[Broiled Fish]*

PSARI TIGANITO *[Fried Fish]*

MARIDES TIGANITES *[Fried Smelts]*

BAKALIAROS VRASTOS *[Boiled Codfish]*

BAKALIAROS SKORDALIA *[Fried Codfish with Garlic Sauce]*

BAKALIAROS YAHNI *[Stewed Codfish]*

PLAKI *[Baked Fish with Vegetables]*

SPETSIOTEKO PSARI *[Baked Fish, Spetsai Style]*

BARBOUNIA STO HARTI *[Red Mullet in Foil]*

SENAGREDA ME PATATES *[Red Snapper with Potatoes]*

SENAGREDA KREA *[Cold Fish Platter]*

OKTAPODI KRASSATO *[Octopus in Wine]*

KALAMARIA YEMISTA *[Stuffed Squid]*

MIDIA PILAFFI *[Mussels Pilaf]*

GARIDES VRASTES *[Boiled Shrimp]*

GARIDES ME SALTSA *[Shrimp in Sauce]*

8 · Fish and Seafood

LIKE THE people of all seabound lands, Greeks make the most of their abundant fish supply. The variety is extensive, the quality excellent, and much of the population is in close enough proximity to the sea to secure it fresh.

Fish is classified as meat under Orthodox religious dietary practice and forbidden on fast days with three exceptions—March 25 (Annunciation and Independence Day), Palm Sunday, and August 6 (Transfiguration Day). The nonvertebrate seafoods such as octopus, squid, cuttlefish, mussels, shrimp, prawns, and crayfish are especially important in Greek cookery as they are served during all fast times except Holy Week.

Not all Greek fish and seafoods are available in American markets. The recipes we give are for the most popular which we have found available in both New York City and Washington, D.C. Squid and mussels must be specially ordered in some markets. As octopus is imported in canned or dried form it should be available in many places. In Greece, crab and lobster are not too plentiful or treated with any special style to justify including them in the recipe collection.

There are four appropriate sauces the Greeks serve over fish—
Lado-Lemono (Oil and Lemon), Savore, Skordalia (Garlic
Sauce), and Mayoneza (Greek Mayonnaise). Recipes for these
are given in Chapter 15.

PSARI TIS SKARAS

[Broiled Fish]

Broiling is the most popular way of cooking fish in Greece and
is usually done over charcoal. The fish is basted with Oil and
Lemon Sauce during cooking with the balance of the sauce poured
over the fish before serving.

4 pounds firm, thick fish fillets or steaks
salt and pepper
1 cup Oil and Lemon Sauce (page 237)

Wash and dry the fish and sprinkle with salt and pepper. Place
on broiler rack and brush with Oil and Lemon Sauce. Broil 5
minutes on each side or until thoroughly cooked. Use sauce for
basting as the fish broils. Place on a platter and pour balance of
sauce over fish. *Serves 8.*

PSARI TIGANITO

[Fried Fish]

Flounder, mackerel, red snapper, salmon, or any firm fish fillet
or steak can be prepared by this recipe and served with a choice
of Savore (page 238), Skordalia (page 238), Mayoneza (page
239), or lemon juice squeezed over the fish followed by pan
drippings, if desired.

2 pounds fish fillets or steaks
salt and pepper

½ *cup flour*
¼ *teaspoon baking powder*
¼ *teaspoon salt*
1 *egg*
2 *teaspoons water*
½ *cup olive oil*

Wash the fish, blot dry, and sprinkle with salt and pepper. Sift together onto wax paper the flour, baking powder, and salt. Beat the egg slightly with the water. Dip the fish pieces in the egg, then roll in flour to coat completely. Heat the oil to sizzling in a large, heavy skillet. Fry the fish slowly, about 5 minutes on each side or until thoroughly cooked and well browned. Drain on paper towels. Prepare desired sauce and serve over the fish. *Serves 4.*

MARIDES TIGANITES

[Fried Smelts]

These small whole fish are coated only with flour. Oil and Lemon or Savore Sauce are served over the fried smelts.

2 *pounds smelts*
salt and pepper
flour for coating
1 *cup olive oil*
juice of 2 lemons

Clean smelts and remove and discard heads and gills. Wash thoroughly. Sprinkle with salt and pepper and coat heavily with flour. Heat olive oil to sizzling in a large skillet, place smelts close together in skillet, and fry on one side until golden brown. Turn carefully to keep whole, cover, and fry over medium flame until other side is well browned and fish is cooked through. Arrange on a platter. Pour lemon juice over them and 2 tablespoons olive oil from the skillet. *Serves 4 to 6.*

Alternate sauce: If Savore Sauce is preferred, eliminate lemon juice and oil over top and follow recipe on page 238.

BAKALIAROS VRASTOS

[Boiled Codfish]

When using salted dry codfish for this or any other recipe, it must first be soaked for 15 hours. Cut the large fillets in serving pieces and cover them completely with water in a large bowl. The water should be changed at intervals, 6 times in all, during the 15 hours. Drain them well before proceeding with recipe. Little or no salt will be necessary.

1 two-pound fillet of codfish, soaked
water to cover
juice of 1 lemon
2 bay leaves
1 cup Oil and Lemon Sauce (page 237) or Greek Mayonnaise (page 239)

Place pieces of soaked fish in a saucepan, cover with water, add lemon juice and bay leaves, and boil 30 minutes or until fish is soft. Drain and place on a platter. Cover with choice of sauce. *Serves 6.*

BAKALIAROS SKORDALIA

[Fried Codfish with Garlic Sauce]

This is a universally popular fish dish in Greece.

1 two-pound fillet of codfish

flour for coating
1 cup olive oil
1 cup Skordalia (Garlic Sauce, page 238)

Cut the codfish in serving pieces and soak according to directions above. Blot dry and coat with flour. No salt is necessary. Heat the oil to sizzling in a heavy skillet and fry the fish over a low flame until cooked through and golden on both sides. Transfer to a platter and cover with Skordalia. *Serves 4 to 6.*

BAKALIAROS YAHNI

[Stewed Codfish]

2 pounds codfish, cut into pieces (salted or fresh)
1 teaspoon salt (omit if using salted codfish)
¼ teaspoon pepper
½ cup olive oil
2 large onions, sliced
1 cup canned tomatoes
½ cup tomato sauce
⅓ cup dry white wine
½ cup water
2 tablespoons wine vinegar
½ cup chopped parsley

If using salted codfish, soak according to directions above. Sprinkle with pepper and also salt if fresh fish. In a large saucepan heat the olive oil and sauté the onion slices until light brown. Add the tomatoes and tomato sauce, cover, and cook 10 minutes. Add the wine, water, vinegar, and fish. Sprinkle parsley over top. Cover and cook 25 minutes, until fish is done and liquid is reduced to a thick sauce. *Serves 6.*

PLAKI

[Baked Fish with Vegetables]

Red snapper, rockfish, fresh or salted codfish, bluefish, or swordfish are suitable for this recipe, either as steaks or large fillets.

2 pounds fish steaks or fillets
6 tablespoons olive oil
⅓ cup dry white wine
juice of 1 lemon
2 teaspoons salt (omit 1 teaspoon for salted codfish)
½ teaspoon pepper
1 package frozen spinach (or ½ pound fresh)
2 bunches scallions, chopped
2 large onions, chopped
2 cups canned tomatoes
¼ cup black currants

Wash and dry the fish and cut into serving pieces. If salted codfish is used, it must have been soaked according to directions on page 78. Pour 1 tablespoon oil and the wine in bottom of a baking dish and arrange fish. Sprinkle with lemon juice, 1 teaspoon salt (omit for salted codfish), ¼ teaspoon pepper, and bake at 350 degrees about 15 minutes.

Defrost the spinach and drain dry. If using fresh spinach, wilt it with boiling water, then drain dry. In a heavy skillet heat the remaining oil, add scallions and onions, and sauté until slightly brown. Add spinach, cook a few minutes, then add tomatoes, currants, remaining salt and pepper, and cook 15 minutes.

Remove fish from oven and spread vegetables over it. Return to oven and bake 30 minutes longer. If sauce becomes watery, spoon out the liquid, thicken with a little flour paste, and return

to baking dish. The thickening must cook at least 10 minutes.
Serves 6.

SPETSIOTEKO PSARI

[Baked Fish, Spetsai Style]

This recipe comes from the island of Spetsai.

2 pounds rockfish or red snapper, cut into 6 steaks
juice of 1 lemon
1 teaspoon salt
¼ teaspoon pepper

SAUCE:
6 tablespoons olive oil
4 onions, finely chopped
3 cups canned tomatoes
⅓ cup dry white wine
1 tablespoon parsley flakes
1 teaspoon salt
¼ teaspoon pepper
1 cup dry toast crumbs, finely ground
juice of 1 lemon

Wash and dry the fish and arrange in a buttered 9x10x2-inch
baking dish. Sprinkle with lemon juice, salt, and pepper, then
set aside for 30 minutes. Bake at 350 degrees for 15 minutes.

Heat the oil in a heavy skillet and sauté the onion until slightly
brown. Add other ingredients except toast crumbs and lemon
juice and simmer until sauce is thick. Spread half the sauce over
the fish and sprinkle with half the crumbs. Return to oven and
bake 15 minutes longer. Spread remaining sauce over fish,
sprinkle with lemon juice and remaining crumbs. Raise oven temperature to 375 degrees and bake another 15 minutes. *Serves 6.*

BARBOUNIA STO HARTI

[Red Mullet in Foil]

2 *pounds red mullet*
salt and pepper
juice of 1 lemon
¼ *cup olive oil*
½ *cup Oil and Lemon Sauce (page 237)*

Clean and wash the fish and sprinkle with salt and pepper. Place in a large bowl, sprinkle with lemon juice, and let stand for 1 hour. Cut pieces of aluminum foil large enough to wrap each fish completely. Rub each fish well with olive oil, place in middle of foil, and sprinkle with a little lemon juice from bottom of bowl. Seal the foil so no steam can escape. Place the wrapped fish on a charcoal grill or in 375-degree oven and cook 20 to 25 minutes. Unwrap carefully, transfer to a plate, and serve with Oil and Lemon Sauce. *Serves 4.*

SENAGREDA ME PATATES

[Red Snapper with Potatoes]

3 *pounds red snapper, cut into serving pieces*
salt and pepper
2¼ *cups water*
3 *small carrots, sliced*
1 *onion, sliced*
1 *stalk celery, cut into pieces*
2 *bay leaves*
½ *cup dry white wine*
2 *tablespoons flour (in paste)*

12 very small boiled potatoes
2 tablespoons chopped parsley
lemon wedges (for garnish)

Clean and wash the fish, sprinkle with salt and pepper, and set aside. In a kettle combine 2 cups of water, carrots, onion, celery, bay leaves, 2 teaspoons salt, and a little pepper. Cover and cook 15 minutes. Add the wine and fish and cook 25 minutes longer or until fish is done but not falling apart. Carefully remove fish to a warm platter so pieces remain whole. Strain the stock. Make a paste of the flour and remaining ¼ cup of water, add to stock and boil gently 5 minutes. Place boiled potatoes around the fish platter. Pour the sauce over the fish and sprinkle parsley over top. Garnish with lemon wedges. *Serves 6.*

Alternate sauce: Greek Mayonnaise (page 239) can be served over the fish in place of the thickened stock.

SENAGREDA KREA

[Cold Fish Platter]

This is often served as a first course at a formal dinner in an Athenian home. It also makes an attractive dish for a buffet.

1 whole red snapper (about 6 pounds)
salt and pepper
juice of 1 lemon
1 onion, chopped
1 carrot, chopped
1 stalk celery, chopped
2 sprigs parsley
2 bay leaves
¼ cup dry white wine
¼ cup olive oil

1 cup water
1½ cups Greek Mayonnaise (page 239)
¼ cup chopped parsley
sliced cooked beets (see Beet Salad, page 53)
sliced cucumbers
Kalamata olives

Wash and dry the fish, sprinkle with salt, pepper, and lemon juice, and let stand 30 minutes. Combine onion, carrot, celery, parsley sprigs, bay leaves, wine, olive oil, and water in a shallow covered pan large enough to take whole fish. (A small roasting pan may be most satisfactory.) Place the fish in pan, cover, and simmer 20 minutes or until fish is cooked through. Do not overcook. Remove the fish carefully to a bread board and cool. Remove head, tail, skin, and bones. Place the whole fillets on a platter and chill well before covering with Greek Mayonnaise. Sprinkle chopped parsley over top. Surround the fish with sliced cooked beets (preferably prepared as Beet Salad), crisp slices of cucumber, and Kalamata olives. *Serves 12.*

OKTAPODI KRASSATO

[Octopus in Wine]

This can be made from fresh, dried, or canned octopus. Fresh octopus needs only to be washed and pounded. The canned is ready to use after being washed well and drained. Soak the dried octopus in cold water for 24 hours, changing the water several times. Drain and dry it, then pound flat.

2 pounds octopus
½ cup olive oil
½ cup grated onion
1½ cups dry red wine (dark preferred)

½ cup tomato sauce
salt and pepper
2 bay leaves
boiling water to cover

Pound the octopus flat, cut into 1-inch pieces, and set aside.
Heat the olive oil in a heavy saucepan. Add the onion and sauté
until brown. Add the wine, tomato sauce, salt, pepper, and bay
leaves. Cover and cook slowly 15 minutes. Add the octopus and
enough boiling water to just cover it. Cover and cook over
medium flame 15 minutes if canned or 30 minutes if fresh or
soaked dried octopus. *Serves 6.*

KALAMARIA YEMISTA

[Stuffed Squid]

12 medium-size squid
salt and pepper
¼ cup olive oil
⅓ cup water
¼ cup dry white wine
¼ cup chopped parsley (for topping)
lemon wedges (for garnish)

STUFFING:
½ cup olive oil
1 cup onions, grated
squid tentacles, chopped
1½ cups canned tomatoes
2 tablespoons chopped parsley
salt and pepper
1 cup warm water
¾ cup rice
¼ cup pignolia nuts (pine nuts)

Prepare the squid by removing soft backbones and ink sacs and pulling off black membranes covering the squid. Cut off heads and discard. Wash thoroughly and drain. Cut off the tentacles and chop fine for use in stuffing. Sprinkle bodies with salt and pepper and set aside while making stuffing.

To make stuffing, heat the oil in a heavy pan. Add the onion and chopped tentacles and sauté until light brown. Add tomatoes, parsley, salt, and pepper, and cook a few minutes. Add the warm water and bring to a boil. Add the rice, cover, and boil gently 18 minutes. Add the pignolia nuts and set aside to cool.

Fill squid cavities with stuffing and close ends securely with toothpicks. Arrange close together in a casserole or Pyrex baking dish. Pour olive oil, water, and wine over them. Bake at 375 degrees for 30 minutes, turning them once during baking. Serve with chopped parsley sprinkled over top and lemon wedges on the side. *Serves 6.*

MIDIA PILAFFI

[Mussels Pilaf]

2 dozen mussels in shells
1 onion, grated
½ cup olive oil
¼ cup cold water
1 cup dry white wine
¼ cup tomato sauce
salt and pepper
warm water to cover
¾ cup rice

Scrub the shells of mussels and put in a kettle with onion, oil, and cold water. Cover and cook over a low flame until shells open. Then add wine, tomato sauce, salt, pepper, and enough warm

water to cover shells. Cover and cook 15 minutes longer. Remove
and shell the mussels. Measure the stock and add water, if necessary, to make 2 cups. Return the mussels to kettle with stock, add
rice, cover, and cook 18 to 20 minutes, or until rice is done.
Serves 4.

GARIDES VRASTES

[Boiled Shrimp]

2 pounds raw shrimp (fresh or frozen)
1 large onion, sliced
1 lemon, sliced
1 tablespoon salt
1 tablespoon mixed pickling spice
2 quarts water

Wash the shrimp and drain. Combine all other ingredients in
a large kettle and bring to a hard boil. Drop in the shrimp, bring
to a boil again, and boil, uncovered, for 10 minutes. Remove
shrimp to colander to drain and cool, then shell and devein.

The boiled shrimp can be broiled (if they are very large) or
fried (the Greeks do it without batter). They can be used cold in
salad (page 55), or as an hors d'oeuvre with dip (page 240).
Boiled shrimp is also called for in the following recipe.

GARIDES ME SALTSA

[Shrimp in Sauce]

1 pound boiled shrimp, shelled and deveined
⅓ cup olive oil
1 cup grated onion

1½ cups canned tomatoes
¾ cup dry white wine
2 tablespoons chopped parsley
2 bay leaves
salt and pepper

Prepare the shrimp according to the recipe for boiled shrimp above. Heat the olive oil, add the onion, and sauté until very light brown. Add the tomatoes, wine, parsley, bay leaves, salt, and pepper. Cover and simmer 20 minutes. Add the shrimp and simmer 15 minutes longer. *Serves 4.*

POULTRY

KOTA GIOUVETSI *[Chicken in Casserole]*

KOTOPOULO TIS HYDRAS *[Chicken in Brandy]*

KOTA KAPAMA *[Chicken in Tomato Sauce]*

KOTA RIGANATI *[Chicken Oregano with Potatoes]*

KOTA ME BAMYES *[Chicken with Okra]*

KOTA ME KARETHIA *[Chicken with Walnut Sauce]*

KOTA ME HILOPITES *[Chicken with Noodles]*

KOTA YAHNI *[Chicken Stew]*

KOTA ATZEM PILAFFI *[Chicken Pilaf with Tomato]*

POULAIREKA PILAFFI *[Poultry Pilaf]*

KOTAS SIKOTAKIA KAI NEFRA ARNESIA KRASSATA *[Chicken Livers and Lamb Kidneys in Wine]*

KOTOPITA *[Chicken Pie]*

PSITE KOTA RIGANATI *[Baked Chicken Oregano]*

YEMISTO GALOPOULO *[Stuffed Turkey]*

PSITO PAPI ME SALTSA PORTOCALE *[Roast Duckling with Orange Sauce]*

YEMISTO PITSOUNI *[Baked Stuffed Squab]*

PITSOUNIA KRASSATA *[Pigeons in Wine]*

9 · Poultry

ONE COULD hardly pass through a Greek village without having to dodge a number of chickens in the roadway. Every family keeps a small flock to supply it with eggs and provide the occasional treat of a chicken dinner. The fowl is flavorful but often a little tough. Therefore, most Greek recipes for chicken are prepared by braising or stewing to tenderize the meat.

Chicken is considered rather special and very appropriate for important occasions. It is customary to serve chicken at an engagement party, and villagers demonstrate their esteem for special guests by killing a chicken for the company meal. A rooster is one of the traditional foods for New Year's Day, and it is taken into the house to be killed for the Greeks believe this brings good luck.

Some village homes have pigeon roosts, small openings high in the outside walls of the house to accommodate the birds raised for food. They are used when small squabs or as full-grown pigeons. Partridge is the most prevalent game bird and is found in many of the larger islands as well as on the mainland.

KOTA GIOUVETSI

[Chicken in Casserole]

This dish takes its name from the utensil in which it is cooked, a special clay baking dish. A covered casserole or other baking dish covered with aluminum foil can be substituted.

1 three-pound frying chicken
salt and pepper
5 tablespoons butter
1 large onion, sliced
2 tablespoons flour
1 cup water
½ cup tomato sauce
1 cup dry white wine
1 cup sliced mushrooms, fresh or canned
1 cup cooked green peas
1 tablespoon chopped parsley (for garnish)

Cut chicken into quarters and sprinkle with salt and pepper. Heat 4 tablespoons of the butter in a large heavy kettle or Dutch oven. Brown the chicken well on all sides. Remove and drain on paper towels. Sauté the onion in the drippings. Make a paste of flour and a little of the water and add to kettle with water, tomato sauce, wine, and a little more salt and pepper. Stir to blend sauce well, return chicken to kettle, cover, and cook over low flame 45 to 50 minutes or until chicken is loose from bone. Remove chicken pieces to a plate and pull largest bones from meat, being careful not to break pieces apart. Butter a 2-quart casserole or baking dish (giouvetsi, if you have one) and arrange the chicken pieces in bottom. In a small skillet sauté the mushrooms in the remaining 1 tablespoon butter a few minutes and distribute around chicken. Pour the peas over the chicken. Strain the sauce over the chicken and vegetables, forcing all through the strainer. Sprinkle parsley over top. Cover and bake at 350 degrees for 20 minutes. *Serves 4.*

KOTOPOULO TIS HYDRAS

[Chicken in Brandy]

Every tourist to Hydra should remember this.

1 three-pound frying chicken
salt and pepper
¼ pound butter
¾ cup brandy
½ cup heavy cream

Wash the chicken, cut into quarters, and sprinkle with salt and pepper. Melt the butter in a heavy skillet and fry the chicken until golden brown. Pour the brandy over the chicken, cover tightly, and simmer 45 minutes. Slowly add the cream and cook 10 minutes longer. *Serves 4.*

KOTA KAPAMA

[Chicken in Tomato Sauce]

This is Arcadian style and a family specialty.

1 three-pound frying chicken
juice of 1 lemon
1 teaspoon salt
¼ teaspoon pepper
1½ teaspoons cinnamon
½ cup vegetable oil
1 tablespoon butter
1 onion, chopped
½ cup dry white wine
⅓ cup boiling water

SAUCE:

1 *tablespoon drippings*
1 *tablespoon flour*
1 *cup water*
1 *cup canned tomatoes*
1 *cup tomato sauce*
¼ *cup dry white wine*
1 *teaspoon salt*
dash of pepper
½ *teaspoon cinnamon*
2 *tablespoons grated kefalotyri cheese (or Parmesan or Romano)*

Cut the chicken into quarters, wash and dry, and place in a bowl. Drip lemon juice over it and sprinkle with salt, pepper, and cinnamon. Let stand for 15 minutes. Heat the oil in a heavy skillet and fry the chicken until golden brown. (Retain 1 tablespoon of drippings in skillet for sauce.) In a large heavy saucepan melt the butter and sauté the onion. Transfer the chicken to saucepan, add the wine, cover, and simmer 15 minutes. Add the boiling water and simmer 15 minutes longer.

To prepare the sauce, make a paste of the flour and a little of the water and combine all the ingredients except cheese in the skillet. Cook gently for 10 minutes, stirring to keep sauce smooth. Add the cheese, then pour the sauce over the chicken, cover, and cook 20 minutes or until chicken is well done. Serve with rice, orzo, or noodles. Top with more grated cheese, or serve yogurt on the side. *Serves 4.*

KOTA RIGANATI

[Chicken Oregano with Potatoes]

This well-known chicken dish is served in the restaurants and tavernes as well as homes throughout Greece.

1 three-pound frying chicken
salt and pepper
¼ cup lemon juice
4 teaspoons oregano
1¼ cups vegetable oil
4 cloves of garlic (or less)
½ cup dry white wine
1 tablespoon flour
1 cup water
1½ cups canned tomatoes
12 very small potatoes

Wash the chicken inside and out, dry, and leave whole. Rub
with salt and pepper, then pour 3 tablespoons of the lemon juice
over whole surface and sprinkle with 2 teaspoons of the oregano.
Let stand for 10 minutes. Heat ¼ cup of the vegetable oil in a
large heavy kettle. Cut the garlic cloves into pieces and sauté,
then add chicken and brown on all sides. Add the wine, cover,
and simmer 10 minutes. Make a paste of the flour and a little of
the water, then combine with balance of water and tomatoes in a
saucepan. Stir and cook for 5 minutes, then add to chicken. Cover
and cook gently for 35 minutes.

While chicken is cooking peel potatoes, place in a bowl, and
season with salt, pepper, the remaining lemon juice, and the remaining oregano. Heat the remaining vegetable oil in a skillet and
brown the potatoes. Drain on paper towels.

After chicken has cooked in the sauce 35 minutes add the
potatoes. If liquid has cooked down too much, add ½ cup boiling
water. Cover and continue cooking 15 minutes or until chicken
and potatoes are done. Skim off any fat. Arrange on a large platter with potatoes surrounding chicken. Spoon sauce over the
top. *Serves 4.*

KOTA ME BAMYES

[Chicken with Okra]

1 three-pound frying chicken
salt and pepper
4 tablespoons butter
1 onion, chopped
½ cup dry white wine
1 cup water
1 tablespoon flour
1 cup tomato sauce
1 pound fresh okra or 1 package frozen
4 tablespoons olive oil or vegetable oil

Wash and cut the chicken into serving pieces. Sprinkle with salt and pepper. In a heavy kettle or Dutch oven melt the butter and sauté the onion. Add the chicken and brown on all sides. Add the wine, cover, and let steam for 10 minutes. Use a little of the water to make a paste of the flour, then blend this with remaining water and tomato sauce in a saucepan. Heat to boiling, then pour over the chicken, cover, and cook 40 minutes.

Treat the okra according to directions on page 62. Heat the 4 tablespoons of oil in skillet and sauté the okra until slightly brown. Drain on paper towels, then add to chicken. If sauce with chicken has cooked down too much, add ½ cup boiling water with the vegetables. Cook together 30 minutes if fresh okra or 20 minutes if frozen. *Serves 4.*

KOTA ME KARETHIA

[Chicken with Walnut Sauce]

This is a good party dish. Serve the chicken and sauce over orzo or rice.

1 *three-pound frying chicken*
salt and pepper
¼ *cup flour*
¼ *cup butter*
1 *small onion, grated*
⅓ *cup dry white wine*
1 *cup boiling water*
2 *tablespoons cornstarch*
1 *cup milk*
2 *egg yolks*
½ *cup finely ground walnuts*
2 *tablespoons chopped parsley (for topping)*

Wash the chicken and cut into serving pieces. Sprinkle with salt and pepper and dredge with flour. Melt the butter in a heavy Dutch oven, add the onion and chicken, and brown lightly on all sides. Add the wine, cover, and simmer for 10 minutes. Add the boiling water, cover, and cook over low flame for 50 minutes. Remove the chicken pieces to a pan, being careful to keep pieces whole. Cover to keep warm. Dissolve the cornstarch in the milk and add slowly to stock in Dutch oven. Beat the egg yolks slightly and add. Cook the sauce a few minutes, stirring as it thickens. Add the ground walnuts and cook 5 minutes longer.

Serve with buttered rice or orzo. Spoon the walnut sauce over the chicken and sprinkle with chopped parsley. *Serves 4 to 6.*

KOTA ME HILOPITES

[Chicken with Noodles]

This is a family dish served in village and city homes.

1 *three-pound frying chicken*
1½ *teaspoons salt*
¼ *teaspoon pepper*

½ *teaspoon cinnamon*
2 *tablespoons flour*
5 *tablespoons butter*
1 *large onion, finely chopped*
¼ *cup dry white wine*
5 *cups boiling water*
¼ *cup cold water*
1 *cup canned tomatoes*
3 *tablespoons tomato sauce*
1 *cup noodles*
¼ *cup grated kefalotyri cheese (or Parmesan or Romano, for topping)*

Wash and cut the chicken into serving pieces. Combine ½ teaspoon salt, little of the pepper, the cinnamon, and 1 tablespoon of the flour and sprinkle over the chicken. In a large heavy kettle melt 4 tablespoons of the butter and sauté the onion. Add chicken and brown slightly on all sides. Add the wine and 2 cups of the boiling water, cover, and simmer 25 minutes.

Make a paste of the remaining 1 tablespoon flour and cold water, combine with tomatoes, tomato sauce, remaining salt, pepper, and butter in a saucepan and cook for 10 minutes. Add to the chicken and cook 15 minutes longer.

Add the remaining 3 cups boiling water to chicken, bring to boil again, and add noodles. Cook 15 to 20 minutes or until noodles are done. Serve with grated cheese on top. *Serves 4 to 6.*

Variation: Orzo can be substituted for noodles and cooked the same length of time.

KOTA YAHNI

[Chicken Stew]

1 *three-pound frying chicken*
salt and pepper

4 tablespoons butter
4 large onions, coarsely grated
¾ cup dry white wine
1½ cups canned tomatoes
½ cup tomato sauce
1 tablespoon flour
¼ cup water
1½ cups hot water

Wash and cut chicken into pieces. Sprinkle with salt and
pepper. In a large heavy kettle or Dutch oven melt the butter.
Add the chicken and brown on all sides. Remove chicken to a
bowl. Add the onions to the butter and sauté until very light
brown. Add half the wine, cover, and simmer a few minutes until
onions are soft. Make a paste of the flour and water. Add the
tomatoes, tomato sauce, and flour paste, and season with salt
and pepper. Cook a few minutes until slightly thick and smooth,
then add the chicken. Pour the balance of the wine and hot
water over it, cover, and simmer 40 to 50 minutes or until chicken
is done. If the sauce becomes too thick add a little more hot water.
There should be at least 1 cup of sauce to serve with the chicken.
Serves 4.

KOTA ATZEM PILAFFI

[Chicken Pilaf with Tomato]

This is a popular family meal. It is served in restaurants as
well as homes.

1 three-pound frying chicken
salt and pepper
6 tablespoons butter
1 large onion, finely chopped

½ cup dry white wine
1 cup canned tomatoes
1 cup tomato sauce
1 cup water
1 teaspoon salt
3 cups boiling water
1 cup rice
yogurt or grated kefalotyri cheese (or Parmesan or Romano,
    for topping)

Wash the chicken, cut into serving pieces, and sprinkle with salt and pepper. Heat 4 tablespoons of the butter in a large heavy kettle, add onion and chicken, and brown on all sides (it may be necessary to do a few pieces at a time). When all pieces are brown add the wine, cover, and let steam for 10 minutes. In a saucepan combine the tomatoes, tomato sauce, water, and salt. Bring to a boil and add to chicken. Cover and cook over a low flame for 40 minutes. Add the boiling water, then the rice, and cook, covered, 20 minutes longer. Heat the remaining butter to sizzling and mix into the pilaf after it is fully cooked. Remove from flame and put aside for a few minutes, then serve with yogurt or grated cheese on top. *Serves 6.*

POULAIREKA PILAFFI

[Poultry Pilaf]

Chicken, capon, or turkey can be used for this version, which has a Near Eastern character.

4 pounds poultry
1 onion, chopped
1 stalk celery, chopped
1 sprig parsley

1 tablespoon salt
¼ teaspoon pepper
3 cups water
1 cup rice
¼ cup pignolia nuts (pine nuts)
2 tablespoons butter
2 tablespoons flour
¾ cup warm milk
¼ cup grated kefalotyri cheese (or Parmesan or Romano)

Wash the fowl and cut into serving pieces. Place in a large
heavy kettle with onion, celery, parsley, 2 teaspoons salt, pepper,
and water. Cover and cook until the meat is loose from bones.
This may take 1 to 2 hours depending on age and toughness of
the foul. Transfer to a platter and remove meat from bones. Strain
and measure the stock and add water to make 3 cups. In a saucepan heat 2 cups stock to boiling. Add the rice and remaining salt
and cook 15 minutes. Add pine nuts and cook 3 to 5 minutes
longer. In another saucepan melt the butter and blend in the
flour. Gradually add 1 cup stock and milk, stirring constantly.
Add poultry. Cook the sauce a few minutes longer, then add the
cheese. Place rice in a deep serving bowl with a well in the center
for the poultry pieces. Pour the sauce over it. If there is excess
sauce serve in a sauce dish on side. *Serves 6.*

KOTAS SIKOTAKIA KAI NEFRA ARNESIA KRASSATA

[Chicken Livers and Lamb Kidneys in Wine]

18 livers from young chickens
6 lamb kidneys, split in half
salt and pepper
4 tablespoons butter

1 small onion, grated
1 clove garlic, finely chopped
1 teaspoon chopped parsley
½ cup dry white wine
2 cups chicken stock or 2 chicken bouillon cubes in 2 cups
   boiling water
1 tablespoon flour

Wash livers and kidneys and dry with paper towels. Season
with salt and pepper. Melt butter in a heavy skillet and fry the
livers for 4 minutes, turning to cook evenly. Transfer to a bowl.
Fry the kidneys, turning to cook evenly, 5 to 6 minutes, and
transfer to a bowl. Brown the onion, garlic, and parsley in the
skillet, then add the wine. Blend a little of the stock with the flour
to make a paste, add to the stock, and heat. Add to skillet and
cook the sauce a few minutes, stirring to keep smooth. Return the
livers and kidneys, cover, and cook over a low flame 15 minutes
or until meat is tender and sauce is thick. Serve with buttered
rice. *Serves 4.*

KOTOPITA

[Chicken Pie]

Read the directions for handling fillo on page 176 before beginning recipe.

1 three-pound whole frying chicken
1 pound onions, sliced
salt and pepper
2 cups water
1 cup warm milk
¾ pound fillo
¾ pound butter, melted

½ cup dry toast crumbs
6 eggs
¾ cup crumbled feta cheese
½ cup grated kefalotyri cheese (or Parmesan or Romano)
½ teaspoon nutmeg

Wash the chicken inside and out. Place in a large kettle with onions, salt, pepper, and water. Cover and cook about 1 hour until meat falls from bones. Remove chicken and set aside to cool. Strain the stock, pass the onions through a sieve, and return the purée to the stock. Bone the chicken and add the meat to the stock. Add the milk and cook all together for 5 minutes.

Line the bottom of a 13x9x2-inch pan with half the fillo sheets, brushing each layer with melted butter. Sprinkle half the crumbs over fillo, then spread the chicken and sauce over it. Cover with balance of crumbs.

In a bowl beat the eggs well and fold in the cheese and nutmeg. Spread this in a layer over the chicken and crumbs. Cover with remaining sheets of fillo, each brushed with melted butter. Pour any remaining butter over the top. Score just through the top layers of fillo into 12 pieces. Bake at 350 degrees for 1 hour. Let stand 30 minutes or longer before cutting. Can be returned to a moderate oven to reheat. *Serves 12.*

PSITE KOTA RIGANATI

[Baked Chicken Oregano]

1 five-pound roasting chicken
½ cup melted butter
juice of 2 lemons
¾ cup dry white wine
1 teaspoon salt

dash of pepper
1 teaspoon oregano
1 clove garlic
½ cup boiling water

Clean the chicken well, inside and out. In a small saucepan combine melted butter, lemon juice, 2 tablespoons of the wine, salt, pepper, and oregano. Brush the mixture inside and outside of chicken. Place garlic clove inside the bird. Put it in a small roasting pan and pour the balance of the basting sauce, balance of wine, and water in the pan. Cover the chicken with aluminum foil and bake at 325 degrees. After 45 minutes lift the foil, and baste the chicken. After another 30 minutes remove the foil, baste again, and continue baking, basting frequently, about 2½ hours in all. Skim the fat from the drippings and pour any remaining sauce over chicken before serving. *Serves 6.*

YEMISTO GALOPOULO

[Stuffed Turkey]

This is a holiday bird served by many on Christmas or New Year's. A large roasting chicken can be prepared by this recipe also. The alternate stuffing made with ground meat can be used in either the turkey or chicken.

1 ten-pound turkey
2 tablespoons melted butter
salt and pepper
juice of 1 lemon
1 cup dry white wine
2 cups stock
1 tablespoon flour

STUFFING:

½ *cup butter*
2 *small onions, chopped*
cooked turkey liver, chopped
2 *cups toasted bread crumbs*
1 *pound chestnuts, roasted and chopped*
½ *cup dark seedless raisins*
2 *stalks celery, chopped*
1 *cup chopped walnuts*
1 *teaspoon sage*
1 *teaspoon salt*
¼ *cup dry white wine*
1 *cup stock*

STOCK:

neck, wing ends, giblets of turkey
1 *onion*
1 *stalk celery*
1 *teaspoon salt*
¼ *teaspoon pepper*
1 *quart water*

Prepare the stock first. Wash neck, wing ends, and giblets and combine in a large saucepan with other ingredients. Cover and cook until meat falls from neck bone. Strain the stock. Retain liver for stuffing.

Wash the turkey inside and out. Rub it with melted butter. Sprinkle with salt, pepper, and lemon juice, and set aside while preparing stuffing.

Now make the stuffing. Melt the butter in a heavy skillet. Sauté the onions until golden. Add the other ingredients and simmer for 10 minutes. Cool before stuffing the bird.

Stuff the turkey, tie legs together, place in a roasting pan. Pour the cup of wine over it, cover with aluminum foil, and bake at 325 degrees for 4 hours.

Mix a little of the stock with the tablespoon of flour, then add to the 2 cups of stock in a saucepan and simmer 5 minutes. Skim the fat from the roasting pan, then pour the hot stock over the turkey. Raise the oven temperature to 375 degrees and roast the turkey, uncovered, 30 minutes longer or until nicely browned. Baste frequently with the stock. *Serves 10.*

ALTERNATE STUFFING (WITH GROUND MEAT):

2 tablespoons butter
1 small onion, grated
1 pound lean ground beef
½ cup dry white wine
1 tablespoon tomato sauce
1 teaspoon salt
¼ teaspoon pepper
¾ pound chestnuts, roasted and chopped
¼ cup pignolia nuts (pine nuts)
1 cup dry toast crumbs
3 tablespoons small dark raisins
2 tablespoons chopped parsley
1 teaspoon sage

Melt the butter in a skillet, add onion and meat, and sauté until slightly brown. Add wine, tomato sauce, salt and pepper, cover, and simmer 15 minutes. Skim off any fat. Add other ingredients and mix together well. Cool before stuffing bird.

PSITO PAPI ME SALTSA PORTOCALE

[Roast Duckling with Orange Sauce]

This is a delicacy rather special to the Greeks. The stuffing absorbs any strong odor of the duck and is discarded before serving.

1 four-to-five-pound duckling
salt and pepper
1 apple, coarsely chopped
1 small onion, coarsely chopped
1 stalk celery, coarsely chopped
1 cup orange juice
rind of 1 orange
1 teaspoon cornstarch
1 tablespoon water

Wash the duckling well inside and out. Sprinkle with salt and pepper. Fill the cavity with mixture of chopped apple, onion, and celery. Place the duckling in a heavy roasting pan. Pour the orange juice over it and surround it with pieces of rind. Cover and bake at 400 degrees for 20 minutes, then reduce heat to 325 degrees and continue baking 2 hours longer. Transfer the duck to a platter and remove and discard the filling. Skim all the fat from the roasting pan. Make a paste of the cornstarch and water and blend with the sauce in the roaster. Return the duck to the roaster. Increase oven heat to 400 degrees and bake, uncovered, 30 minutes longer or until brown. Baste every 5 minutes with sauce in pan. *Serves 4 to 6.*

YEMISTO PITSOUNI

[Baked Stuffed Squab]

Squab is served in wayside taverns more often than in the cities and is often cooked on a spit over charcoal without the dressing. Use large squab or pigeons to stuff because the small ones do not have a large enough cavity.

4 squab, one and one quarter pounds each
¼ cup olive oil

1 teaspoon oregano
salt and pepper
1 cup dry white wine

STUFFING:
2 tablespoons butter
1 onion, finely chopped
1 stalk celery, chopped
livers from squab, chopped
1 cup finely grated bread crumbs
1 teaspoon salt
10 black olives, finely chopped
¼ cup dry white wine

Clean and wash the squab, then prepare the stuffing. Melt butter in a skillet, add onion, celery, and livers and sauté slowly until tender and slightly brown. Add the bread crumbs, salt, olives, and wine and mix together well.

Stuff the squab and close openings with small skewers. Rub the outsides with olive oil and sprinkle with oregano, salt, and pepper. Place in a baking pan and pour wine over them. Cover and bake at 350 degrees 45 minutes. Remove cover and continue baking 15 minutes longer, basting often. *Serves 4.*

PITSOUNIA KRASSATA

[Pigeons in Wine]

A little taverna on the grounds of the Church of the Virgin in Tegea in the Peloponnesus is famous for this speciality. The taverna operates from Easter Week through the summer season for the benefit of the church and is the scene of a colorful festival for Assumption Day, August 15.

3 pigeons, one and one-half to two pounds each
salt and pepper
¼ cup butter
¼ cup tomato sauce
¼ cup water
1 cup dry white wine
dash of cinnamon
pinch of sugar

Wash the pigeons, cut in half, and sprinkle with salt and pepper. Melt the butter in a large heavy kettle or Dutch oven. Brown the pigeons on all sides, then transfer to a plate. Add the other ingredients to the kettle, including a little more salt and pepper, and simmer a few minutes. Return the pigeons to the kettle, cover tightly, and simmer until birds are tender. *Serves 6.*

Note: Partridge can be cooked this way also.

MEATS

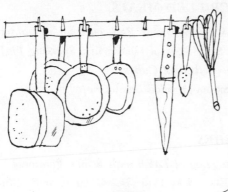

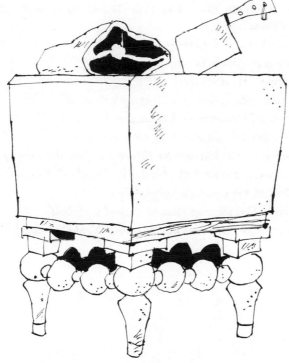

BARBECUED OR GRILLED MEATS:

ARNI STIN SOUVLA *[Whole Lamb Barbecued on an Outdoor Spit]*

GOUROUNOPOULO STIN SOUVLA *[Barbecued Suckling Pig]*

SOUVLAKIA *[Barbecued Meat Cubes]*

BREEZOLES STIN SKARA *[Broiled Lamb Chops]*

BAKED MEAT DISHES:

ARNI ME PATATES *[Leg of Lamb with Brown Potatoes]*

PSITO ARNI ME ELIES KAI TYRI *[Baked Lamb with Olives and Cheese]*

VODINO ROLLO *[Marinated Flank Steak]*

KLEPHTEKO *[Meat in Aluminum Foil]*

KEFTEDES *[Meat Patties]*

MOUSSAKA *[Eggplant and Meat with Custard]*

PASTICHIO *[Macaroni and Meat with Custard]*

KANELONIA *[Filled Pancakes with Sauce]*

KREATOPITA CEPHALONITIKI *[Meat Pie, Island Version]*

KREATOPITA YANNIOTIKI *[Meat Pie, Mainland Version]*

TSIOPANIKI PITA *[Greek Shepherd's Pie]*

YEMISTES MELIDZANES *[Baked Stuffed Eggplant]*

GIOUVETSI ME KRETHARAKE *[Lamb or Veal Casserole]*

STEWED OR BRAISED MEAT DISHES:

ARNI Y VEDELO YAHNI *[Basic Lamb or Veal Stew]*

PILAFFI TAS KEBAB *[Meat with Tomato Sauce over Rice]*

ATZEM PILAFFI *[Lamb Pilaf with Tomato]*

STEFADO *[Beef Braised with Onion]*

VODINO ME KASTANA *[Beef with Chestnuts]*

KREAS KRASSATO *[Steak in Wine]*

ARNI KRASSATO *[Lamb Braised in Wine]*

ARNI BREEZOLES ME SALTSA *[Lamb Chops in Sauce]*

ZAKINTHOU BREEZOLES *[Smothered Chops, Ionian Style]*

VEDELO KRASSATO *[Veal Rolls with Bacon in Wine]*

SOUTZOUKAKIA SMYRNEIKA *[Meat Rolls in Sauce]*

KREAS SALTSA *[Meat Sauce for Spaghetti]*

DOLMADES *[Meat Wrapped in Grape Leaves]*

LAHANIKA YEMISTA ME ARNI *[Vegetables Stuffed with Lamb]*

HIRINO ME LAHANO *[Pork with Cabbage]*

KOUNELI STEFADO *[Rabbit Stew]*

KOUNELI ME SKORDALIA *[Rabbit with Garlic Sauce]*

10 · Meats

LAMB IS by far the most popular and plentiful meat in Greece. Veal is generally available, and also beef, though in lesser quantity. Pork is occasionally served but seems to be favored as a suckling pig barbecued whole on a spit. Rarely is meat smoked for such products as ham or bacon. Chicken, fish, and game are frequent substitutes for meat.

Barbecuing over charcoal is an ancient and very satisfactory method of cooking meat which can be done with the crudest of equipment. The Greeks claim to have first conceived the idea of grinding or chopping meat, pointing out that some of their most typical dishes such as Moussaka, Pastichio, and Keftedes use meat in this form. It was chopped by working two sharp knives continually across the meat at cross angles.

Meat is often marinated in wine or a combination of marinade ingredients to absorb flavor and become tenderized. If sprinkled with lemon juice and set aside for 15 minutes or more before cooking it will be more tender and flavorful.

Once meat has been heated, cold liquid should never be added to the pot or it will toughen the meat. Slow cooking minimizes shrinkage and produces more flavorful food. When cooking lamb or veal by dry heat such as oven-roasting or over an open fire, the meat should be basted often to keep it moist.

Greek cookery includes many combination dishes that make perfect one-dish meals. Some, such as those with Avgolemono Sauce, must be served at once. Many of the baked dishes are improved if they stand for a while after baking to set firmly before they are served. This is especially true of Moussaka and Pastichio which contain baked custard sauce. They can be reheated in a a slow oven just before serving.

Unfortunately many of the more elaborate dishes made of many parts cannot be satisfactorily cut down to serve only four people. The total quantity of all the parts, even in the smallest amount possible to give a dish its proper character and flavor, is inevitably sufficient to serve 8, 10, or 12 people.

Greek cooks give special attention to the preparation of lamb and will use it only when young and tender, never as mutton. Therefore, it is primarily a food of winter and early spring and has always been associated with the festive occasions of Christmas, the two weeks of Carnival, and Easter. The cooking of whole lambs out-of-doors is a man's job and one that attracts spectator interest. A visitor never forgets this colorful Greek tradition.

When using less-choice cuts of lamb it is advisable to treat the meat first to remove any strong odor or taste. For shanks, shoulders, and other economy cuts follow these directions before proceeding with a recipe:

To treat economy cuts of lamb—Place the meat in a deep kettle, add enough cold water to cover the meat, and sprinkle with 2 tablespoons of salt. Heat until the water is scalding, then pour it out. Rinse the meat with more scalding water and drain dry.

BARBECUED OR GRILLED MEATS

ARNI STIN SOUVLA

[Whole Lamb Barbecued on an Outdoor Spit]

This is most famous as the meat of the Easter meal, but whole lambs are often cooked to serve to large crowds. Roadside restaurants specialize in this and cut individual servings right from the spit.

1 whole lamb (about 30 pounds)
¾ cup salt
3 tablespoons pepper
1 pound butter, melted
juice of 4 lemons
2 tablespoons oregano

Wash, clean, and dry the lamb. Salt and pepper the inside, then run the long spit through the body and tie the legs. Sew together the opening of cavity. Rub the outside with the remaining salt and pepper. Combine the butter, lemon juice, and oregano and use a third of the mixture to rub over the lamb. Place it in the rack over an open charcoal fire. The fire should be banked to concentrate heat under thighs and shoulders. Keep the spit turning slowly. A motorized spit makes the job easy, but it is done by hand in Greece.

Using a 30-inch stick with thick layers of cheesecloth wrapped and fastened to the end, baste the lamb with the remaining mixture at hour intervals. It will take up to 8 hours to cook, depending on size and heat of fire.

When the lamb is done place it on a large wooden table covered with heavy brown paper. Carve the legs first, then remove the spit, and carve into serving pieces. *Serves 25 to 30.*

GOUROUNOPOULO STIN SOUVLA

[Barbecued Suckling Pig]

In Greece this is the traditional meat for Assumption Day, August 15, and is always cooked outdoors on a spit over a charcoal fire. A suckling pig is usually too large to cook in an oven rotisserie, but should be cooked on a motorized spit. This is very rich meat.

1 whole suckling pig (about 15 pounds)
⅓ cup salt
1 tablespoon pepper
½ cup olive oil
juice of 2 lemons

Clean and wash the pig thoroughly inside and out. Rub the inner cavity with some of the salt and pepper. Insert spit through length of pig. Tie the legs and open parts of the body and make certain it is secure on the spit. Use ¼ cup of the olive oil to rub over entire surface of the pig, then sprinkle with more of the salt and pepper. Place the spit on notch of rack farthest from fire and cook with the spit rotating for 2 hours.

In the meantime wrap the end of a 30-inch stick with many layers of cheesecloth and tie on securely. This will be used to apply basting mixture. Combine the remaining ¼ cup olive oil with lemon juice and any remaining salt and pepper.

After 2 hours cooking, move the spit closer to the fire and baste often. The skin will become very crisp. Cook with spit rotating continually for 6 hours in all. Transfer to a large tray and remove spit before carving. *Serves 8 to 10.*

SOUVLAKIA

[Barbecued Meat Cubes]

Barbecued pieces of meat are a popular snack sold by vendors in many places in Greece. This recipe is intended as an entrée.

1 pound lamb or veal cut from leg
4 ounces sweetbreads (or additional ½ pound meat)
¼ cup olive oil
½ cup dry white wine
¼ cup lemon juice
2 tablespoons wine vinegar
1 tablespoon oregano
1 teaspoon salt
¼ teaspoon pepper
2 cloves garlic, chopped
1 small onion, chopped

Cut the lamb into 2-inch cubes. Cut sweetbreads in 8 pieces. Using four 8-inch skewers, arrange the meat, alternating kinds.

In a wide-based bowl combine the remaining ingredients to make a marinade. Soak the meat in this at least 12 hours, keeping refrigerated. Turn it occasionally.

Place the skewered meat on broiler pan, place on farthest rack from flame, and broil for 50 minutes. Baste it with the marinade and turn it every 15 minutes. This dish can also be cooked on an outdoor rotisserie with the meat arranged on one large spit. If this is done, keep the heat low and allow 2 hours cooking time. Baste often. *Serves 4.*

BREEZOLES STIN SKARA

[Broiled Lamb Chops]

Meat cooked over charcoal has been a specialty of Greek villagers for many centuries. These instructions apply for outdoor grilling or in an oven broiler.

8 *loin lamb chops*
¼ *cup butter*
juice of ½ lemon
1 *teaspoon salt*
¼ *teaspoon pepper*
1 *teaspoon oregano*

Place chops on medium rack of broiler or grill. In a small saucepan melt the butter and add all other ingredients. When chops begin to sizzle brush generously with the butter mixture. Turn after 5 to 6 minutes and brush other side generously. Continue cooking until done (12 to 15 minutes in all for average chops). If more butter remains, brush again before last few minutes of cooking. *Serves 4.*

BAKED MEAT DISHES

ARNI ME PATATES

[Leg of Lamb with Brown Potatoes]

1 *four-pound leg of lamb*
2 *cloves garlic*
salt and pepper
3 *tablespoons melted butter*
juice of ½ lemon

1 *onion, finely chopped*
1 *cup dry white wine*
½ *cup water*
½ *cup vegetable oil*
18 *very small white potatoes*

Wash the lamb well, slit in four places, and insert pieces of garlic. Season with salt and pepper. Combine melted butter and lemon juice and brush over the lamb. Place in a roasting pan with a lid, add the chopped onion, wine, and water. Cover and bake at 325 degrees for 2 hours. Remove the lid, increase the heat to 375 degrees, and continue baking for 1 hour, basting every 15 minutes. Transfer to a platter and cover to keep warm.

In a skillet heat the vegetable oil to sizzling, then fry the potatoes until golden brown. Skim the fat from the meat pan and add the potatoes to the meat drippings. Bake them, uncovered, at 375 degrees for 30 minutes or until cooked through. Arrange the potatoes on the platter around the lamb. *Serves 6 to 8.*

PSITO ARNI ME ELIES KAI TYRI

[Baked Lamb with Olives and Cheese]

1 *four-pound leg of lamb*
3 *tablespoons butter*
garlic salt
pepper
1 *onion, chopped*
1 *cup dry red wine*
1 *cup boiling water*
1 *tablespoon flour*
¼ *cup cold water*
12 *small whole potatoes*

12 small whole onions
½ cup vegetable oil
8 pieces kefalotyri cheese in ½-inch cubes
12 large black olives

Rub the lamb with butter, garlic salt, and pepper. In a covered roasting pan sear the meat over medium flame on the stove top until well browned. Add chopped onion and brown slightly, then add the wine and boiling water. Cover the roaster and bake in a pre-heated oven at 325 degrees for 2½ hours.

Remove roasting pan from oven and transfer stock to a saucepan. Skim off the fat. Make a paste of the flour and water, stir into the stock, and cook 5 minutes, stirring as it thickens.

Wash and peel the potatoes and onions. Heat the oil in a skillet until sizzling. Fry the vegetables until brown.

Make eight slits in the leg of lamb and insert a piece of cheese in each. Pour the thickened stock over the lamb in the roasting pan. Surround the meat with olives, potatoes, and onions. Return to oven, uncovered, raise the temperature to 375 degrees, and bake 40 minutes longer, basting often to keep moist. *Serves 6 to 8.*

VODINO ROLLO

[Marinated Flank Steak]

This is modern Athenian cooking.

1 pound flank beefsteak
1 teaspoon salt
¼ teaspoon pepper
1 teaspoon oregano
2 onions, grated
½ pound lamb livers

4 lamb kidneys
¼ cup olive oil
¼ cup lemon juice
¼ cup dry red wine

Pound the steak flat and sprinkle with salt, pepper, and oregano. Spread the grated onion over the steak. Cut the livers and kidneys in small pieces and distribute over steak. Roll the steak and tie at each end and in center. Place in a shallow Pyrex baking dish. Combine the oil, lemon juice, and wine and pour over the steak roll. Cover the dish with aluminum foil and place in refrigerator to marinate for 12 to 24 hours. Remove from refrigerator several hours before cooking to bring to room temperature. Turn the meat over in the marinade. Bake it, uncovered, at 375 degrees for 1 hour, basting often. Cut in slices to serve. *Serves 4.*

KLEPHTEKO

[Meat in Aluminum Foil]

This is also referred to as "Thieves' Meat," the method of cooking having originated during the Turkish occupation when rebellious Greeks roamed the mountains and often had to steal their food from the Turks. The meat was wrapped in skins so that the cooking odor would not escape and reveal their hide-outs. Lamb chops, beefsteak, ground beef, veal cutlet, pork tenderloin, and chicken can be prepared this way.

4 large thick chops (about 2 pounds)
2 teaspoons salt
½ teaspoon pepper
juice of 1 lemon
4 tablespoons butter

2 *large onions, chopped*
1 *bunch scallions, cut in 1-inch pieces*
1 *cup canned tomatoes*
3 *tablespoons dry wine*
½ *teaspoon dill seed*
2 *tablespoons vegetable oil*
4 *large slices feta cheese*

Sprinkle meat with 1 teaspoon of the salt, a little of the pepper, and lemon juice, and let stand for 1 hour. Melt butter in a skillet, sauté onions and scallions until brown. If they are tough, add ⅓ cup water, cover, and simmer until water is absorbed. Add the tomatoes, wine, remaining salt and pepper, and the dill seed. Cover and cook until sauce is thick. Remove from flame and cool.

In another skillet brown the chops in the oil. Cut 4 pieces of foil large enough to wrap each piece of meat completely. Place meat in center of foil, spoon some of the sauce over it, and cover with a slice of cheese. Fold the foil around the meat and seal. Place on a baking sheet and bake at 350 degrees for 1½ hours for lamb, 2 hours for pork or thick beef, 50 minutes for chicken or thin veal cutlet. *Serves 4.*

KEFTEDES

[Meat Patties]

These are Greek hamburgers, which are popular for informal meals.

1 *pound ground chuck beef*
½ *pound lean ground pork*
1 *onion, grated*

2 eggs

1 tablespoon tomato sauce

1½ teaspoons salt

¼ teaspoon pepper

¼ teaspoon cinnamon

1 teaspoon crushed mint leaves

½ teaspoon oregano

3 slices bread, moistened

½ teaspoon baking soda

¼ cup dry red wine

SAUCE:

drippings from meat

2 teaspoons flour

¼ cup water

1 cup tomato sauce

juice of 1 lemon

¼ cup dry red wine

1 teaspoon oregano

1 teaspoon salt

dash of pepper

2 tablespoons grated kefalotyri cheese (or Parmesan or
Romano)

Combine the meat, onion, eggs, tomato sauce, and seasonings.
Tear the moistened bread in pieces and add. Dissolve the baking
soda in the wine and add. Mix together well and shape into
round patties. Place in a greased shallow baking pan and bake
at 375 degrees 30 to 35 minutes, turning after 15 minutes. Drain
drippings and reserve for sauce.

Transfer meat drippings to a saucepan. Make a paste of flour
and water and add to drippings along with all other ingredients.
Cook, stirring constantly, until sauce is thick. Serve over baked
meat patties. *Serves 6.*

MOUSSAKA

[Eggplant and Meat with Custard]

This is probably the best known of all Greek dishes.

4 large eggplants
flour for coating
½ cup vegetable oil

MEAT SAUCE:
2 tablespoons butter
1 onion, finely chopped
1½ pounds ground chuck beef
½ pound lean ground pork
1 tablespoon salt
½ teaspoon pepper
¼ teaspoon nutmeg
2 tablespoons chopped parsley
3 tablespoons tomato sauce
1 cup dry red wine
½ cup boiling water
2 eggs
1 cup grated kefalotyri cheese (or Parmesan or Romano)
2 slices dry toast, grated

CREAM SAUCE:
¼ cup butter
2 tablespoons flour
¼ cup cold milk
2¾ cups warm milk
1 cup half-and-half cream
3 eggs plus 3 yolks

1 teaspoon salt
½ teaspoon nutmeg
⅓ cup grated kefalotyri cheese (or Parmesan or Romano)

TOPPING:

⅓ cup grated kefalotyri cheese (for between layers and top)

Treat the eggplants according to directions on page 62. They should be cut in ¼-inch-thick slices. Coat the slices with flour. Heat the vegetable oil in a skillet and fry eggplant until golden brown. Drain on paper towels.

Sauté the onion in butter, add the ground meat, and brown well. Add salt, pepper, nutmeg, parsley, tomato sauce, wine, and boiling water. Cover and cook until the sauce thickens. Beat the eggs and add. Add cheese and half the grated toast and mix well.

Grease a 12x10x3-inch baking pan. Spread remaining half of toast crumbs over bottom. Arrange half the eggplant over crumbs. Cover with meat sauce, then sprinkle 2 tablespoons cheese from topping over it. Cover this with the remaining eggplant.

To make cream sauce, melt butter in a saucepan. Make a paste of the flour and cold milk and add the flour paste, warm milk, and cream to the pan. Blend until smooth and simmer about 15 minutes. Remove from flame and add beaten eggs while stirring the sauce vigorously. Stir in the salt, nutmeg, and ⅓ cup cheese. Pour over the eggplant dish. Sprinkle top with remaining cheese. Bake at 375 degrees for 45 minutes. Let the dish stand for 20 minutes before serving. *Serves 10 to 12.*

PASTICHIO

[Macaroni and Meat with Custard]

This is a well-known and typically Greek dish.

MEAT SAUCE:

1 tablespoon butter
1 onion, grated

1 *pound lean ground chuck beef*
1 *teaspoon salt*
¼ *teaspoon pepper*
¼ *teaspoon nutmeg*
½ *cup dry white wine*
¼ *cup tomato sauce*
½ *cup boiling water*
2 *slices dry toast, grated*
¼ *cup grated kefalotyri cheese (or Parmesan or Romano)*

MACARONI:

½ *pound macaroni in whole long pieces*
3 *quarts boiling water*
1 *tablespoon salt*
¼ *cup butter*
2 *eggs, slightly beaten*
½ *cup grated kefalotyri cheese (or Parmesan or Romano)*

CREAM SAUCE:

¼ *cup butter*
1 *tablespoon flour*
4 *cups milk*
1 *teaspoon salt*
¼ *teaspoon nutmeg*
3 *whole eggs plus 3 yolks*
¼ *cup grated kefalotyri cheese (or Parmesan or Romano)*

TOPPING:

1 *cup grated kefalotyri cheese (or Parmesan or Romano, for
between layers and top)*

In a heavy skillet melt the butter, sauté the onion a few minutes, then add meat. Break up the meat with a fork as it browns so
there are no lumps. Drain off the fat, then add salt, pepper, nutmeg, and wine. Cover and simmer 5 minutes. Mix tomato sauce

with boiling water and add. Cover and simmer 45 minutes. Remove from flame, stir in grated toast and cheese, and mix well. Set aside.

Break macaroni sticks in half and add to boiling water with salt. Boil for 15 to 18 minutes (should be a little undercooked). Pour out the water, fill pan with scalding water to wash away starch, then pour into a colander to drain. Melt butter in the same pan, return the drained macaroni and stir to mix butter through it. Add the slightly beaten eggs and cheese and stir until well mixed. Set aside.

Melt butter for cream sauce in a saucepan. Make flour into a paste with a little of the milk, and add flour paste, milk, salt, and nutmeg to saucepan. Heat, stirring constantly, until milk comes to a boil, then remove from heat. Beat eggs and yolks well and add to cream sauce, beating to keep smooth. Add cheese and beat again until smooth.

Use a buttered 8x8x2-inch pan (must be this deep), and assemble layers as follows:

½ macaroni
¼ cup grated cheese
all the meat sauce
4 tablespoons cream sauce
balance of macaroni
¼ cup grated cheese
balance of cream sauce
balance of grated cheese

Bake at 350 degrees for 40 minutes or until knife inserted in center comes out clean. Let stand in a warm place, uncovered, for 2 hours to become firmly set before serving. Can be returned to a warm oven for a few minutes to reheat. *Serves 8 to 10.*

Note: Keep leftovers refrigerated and reheat in a slow oven with a little milk in bottom of pan.

KANELONIA

[Filled Pancakes with Sauce]

This dish reflects Italian influence.

FILLING:
2 *tablespoons butter*
1 *small onion, grated*
½ *pound ground beef*
salt and pepper
dash of nutmeg
1 *teaspoon chopped parsley*
¼ *cup tomato sauce*
2 *tablespoons dry red wine*
1 *egg*
1 *hard-boiled egg, grated*
1 *tablespoon dry toast crumbs*
¼ *cup grated kefalotyri cheese (or Parmesan or Romano)*

SAUCE:
1 *cup meat stock or bouillon*
1 *teaspoon flour*
¾ *cup tomato sauce*
¼ *cup dry red wine*
1 *teaspoon butter*
dash of nutmeg
salt and pepper
¼ *teaspoon sugar*

PANCAKES:
2 *eggs*
2 *cups milk*
1 *teaspoon olive oil*

¾ cup sifted flour
½ teaspoon baking powder
1 teaspoon salt
dash of nutmeg
2 tablespoons melted butter
4 tablespoons grated kefalotyri cheese (or Parmesan or
   Romano)

Make the filling first. Melt butter in a skillet, add onion and
meat, and brown well. Add salt, pepper, nutmeg, parsley, tomato
sauce, and wine. Mix together well and simmer for 5 minutes.
Add the raw egg, cooked egg, toast crumbs, and cheese. Stir the
mixture well and cook over low flame 30 minutes. Mixture will
be very thick. Set aside until pancakes are ready.

Next make the sauce. Blend a little of meat stock with flour
into a paste, then combine with all other ingredients in a saucepan and let simmer while making the pancakes.

In a large bowl beat the eggs slightly, add the milk and olive
oil. Sift the dry ingredients together, then sift them into the
liquid mixture and mix well. On a hot, lightly greased skillet fry
the pancakes on each side until golden brown, making each about
the size of a saucer. Transfer the cooked pancakes to a bread
board.

Put 1 to 1½ tablespoons filling on each pancake, roll up, and
place on a greased cookie sheet. Brush tops with butter and
sprinkle with grated cheese. Bake in 375-degree oven until tops
are nicely browned. Serve hot with sauce poured over them.
Serves 6.

KREATOPITA CEPHALONITIKI

[Meat Pie, Island Version]

This recipe from one of the Ionian Islands is a traditional dish
for Ascension Day. See directions for handling fillo on page 176.
Homemade Pastry Dough (page 243) can be substituted for fillo.

½ leg of lamb (about 2½ pounds)
2 onions, chopped
2 teaspoons salt
¼ teaspoon pepper
cold water to cover
¼ cup rice
1 tablespoon butter
2 cloves garlic
¼ cup dry red wine
1 teaspoon finely ground orange rind
½ teaspoon crushed dry mint
½ teaspoon crushed dry parsley
¼ teaspoon cinnamon
3 tablespoons tomato sauce
2 small boiled potatoes, diced
½ cup crumbled feta cheese
½ cup grated kefalotyri cheese (or Parmesan or Romano)
½ pound fillo
½ pound butter, melted
4 hard-boiled eggs, sliced

Wash meat and place in a heavy kettle or Dutch oven. Add half of the chopped onion, salt, pepper, and enough water to cover meat. Cover and cook over a medium flame 1½ to 2 hours or until tender. Skim off the fat. Place the meat on a platter to cool. Measure the stock and add water, if necessary, to make 2 cups.

In a saucepan combine 1 cup stock and rice, cover, and boil for 10 minutes. Melt the butter in a skillet and sauté the remaining onion and garlic until golden. Cut the cooked lamb into 1-inch cubes. In a bowl combine the lamb, partially cooked rice, sautéed onion and garlic, remaining cup of stock, wine, orange rind, mint, parsley, cinnamon, tomato sauce, diced potatoes, feta and grated cheese. Mix together well.

Butter an 8x8x2-inch Pyrex dish. Line bottom with half the fillo sheets, each brushed with butter. Cover with filling, then arrange sliced eggs over top. Cover with remaining sheets of fillo, each brushed with butter. Pour any remaining butter over top. Score through top layers of fillo into eight pieces.

If using homemade crust, use one layer on bottom and one on top, each brushed with butter.

Bake at 350 degrees for 45 minutes. Remove from oven and let stand 15 minutes before cutting, then serve immediately. *Serves 8.*

KREATOPITA YANNIOTIKI

[Meat Pie, Mainland Version]

This recipe is from a town near the Albanian border. It can be made with Homemade Pastry Dough (page 243) if fillo is not available. See directions for handling fillo on page 176.

1 tablespoon butter
½ cup grated onion
1 pound ground meat from lamb shanks
salt and pepper
½ teaspoon parsley
1 teaspoon cinnamon
2 tablespoons tomato sauce
2 cups lamb stock (see Zoumos, page 39)
4 slices dry toast
2 cups milk
4 eggs
½ cup grated kefalotyri cheese (or Parmesan or Romano)
½ pound fillo
½ pound butter, melted

Melt the butter in a large kettle, add onion and ground meat, and brown well. Drain off the fat, then add salt, pepper, parsley, cinnamon, tomato sauce, and meat stock. Cover and simmer 45 minutes. Soak the toast in the milk to soften, then mash to a soft paste and add to meat sauce, blending well. Beat the eggs until thick and creamy and fold the cheese into them.

Line the bottom of an 8x8x2-inch Pyrex dish with half the fillo, brushing each layer with melted butter. Spread the meat sauce over the pastry, then cover with egg and cheese mixture. Cover with remaining fillo sheets, each brushed with butter. Pour any remaining butter over top. Cut through top layers of fillo to score into eight pieces.

If using homemade crust use one layer on bottom and one on top, each brushed with butter.

Bake at 350 degrees for 45 minutes. Remove from oven and let stand 15 minutes before cutting, then serve immediately. *Serves 8.*

TSIOPANIKI PITA

[Greek Shepherd's Pie]

3 medium-size potatoes
3 tablespoons butter
2 small onions, chopped
1 pound lean ground beef or lamb
2 tablespoons tomato sauce
¼ cup dry wine
2 teaspoons salt
½ teaspoon pepper
½ teaspoon nutmeg
¼ cup light cream
½ cup grated kefalotyri cheese (or Parmesan or Romano)

Scrub the potatoes and boil them whole in their skins. While they are cooking prepare the meat sauce.

Melt 1 tablespoon of the butter in a heavy saucepan. Add the onion and sauté until golden. Then add the meat and stir until it is well browned. Add the tomato sauce, wine, 1 teaspoon of the salt, pepper, and nutmeg. Cover and cook 20 minutes.

When the potatoes are done, peel and mash them in a bowl. Warm the cream and add along with remaining butter and salt. Mix well with a rotary beater.

Butter a 9-inch round casserole. Spread half the potatoes over the bottom, cover with meat sauce, and spread remaining potatoes on top. Sprinkle with grated cheese. Bake at 350 degrees for 30 minutes or until potatoes are browned. *Serves 6.*

YEMISTES MELIDZANES

[Baked Stuffed Eggplant]

4 small eggplants (about 5-inches long)
2 tablespoons butter or olive oil
1 onion, chopped
1 pound ground beef
½ cup dry wine
2 teaspoons salt
¼ teaspoon pepper
1 teaspoon parsley flakes
½ cup water

SAUCE:

1 egg
½ cup grated kefalotyri cheese (or Parmesan or Romano)
½ cup milk
¼ teaspoon salt
dash of pepper

Cut eggplants in half lengthwise and scoop out centers but leave unpeeled. Retain centers for filling. Treat eggplant shells and centers according to directions on page 62.

Heat the butter or oil in a skillet, add onion and meat, and brown well. Chop the treated eggplant centers and add, then add wine and seasonings. Cover and simmer 15 minutes. Allow to cool slightly and skim off any fat. Stuff the eggplant shells and place them in a baking pan. Put ½ cup water in the bottom of the pan and bake at 350 degrees for 40 minutes.

Beat the egg, add grated cheese, milk, salt, and pepper and mix together well. Pour this over the stuffed eggplant and brown under the broiler. *Serves 4.*

GIOUVETSI ME KRETHARAKE

[Lamb or Veal Casserole]

The Greeks make this in a special clay cooking utensil called a giouvetsi, but a covered roasting pan is a satisfactory substitute.

1 three-pound half leg of lamb or rump veal roast
salt and pepper
garlic salt
1 small onion, chopped
½ cup dry red wine
2 cups water
1½ cups canned tomatoes
4 cups boiling water
1 tablespoon salt
1½ cups orzo
½ cup grated kefalotyri cheese
    (or Parmesan or Romano)

Season the meat with salt, pepper, and garlic salt. Place in a roasting pan and surround with chopped onion. Pour wine over it and pour 2 cups of water in bottom of pan. Cover and bake at 325 degrees for 2 hours. Remove cover, raise heat to 400 degrees, and bake 30 minutes longer, basting often. Place meat on platter and cover to keep warm.

Skim fat from roaster. To remaining stock add tomatoes, boiling water, and salt. Return to 400-degree oven and let liquids reach boiling point. Add the orzo and cook, uncovered, in oven for 20 minutes. All moisture should be absorbed. Surround meat with orzo and sprinkle cheese over top. *Serves 6.*

Variation: Spaghetti or noodles can be substituted for orzo.

STEWED OR BRAISED MEAT DISHES

ARNI Y VEDELO YAHNI

[Basic Lamb or Veal Stew]

This recipe adapts to two basic versions—with *Tomato Sauce* or with *Avgolemono Sauce*. Further variation is made with a wide selection of vegetables that are suitable to one version or the other.

Use the *Tomato Sauce* version for the following:

LAMB OR VEAL WITH ONIONS

LAMB OR VEAL WITH POTATOES

LAMB OR VEAL WITH GREEN BEANS

LAMB OR VEAL WITH GREEN PEAS

LAMB OR VEAL WITH CAULIFLOWER

LAMB OR VEAL WITH OKRA

LAMB OR VEAL WITH ZUCCHINI

LAMB OR VEAL WITH EGGPLANT

PILAFFE TAS KEBAB

Use the *Avgolemono Sauce* version for the following:

LAMB WITH ARTICHOKE HEARTS

LAMB WITH CELERY

LAMB WITH ENDIVE

LAMB WITH DANDELION GREENS

3 *pounds lamb or veal shoulder*
2 *tablespoons butter (4 tablespoons for veal)*
1 *onion, chopped*
½ *cup dry red or white wine (white only for Avgolemono*
    version)
4 *cups boiling water*
1 *tablespoon salt*
¼ *teaspoon pepper*

Cut meat into 2-inch cubes. If lamb, treat according to directions on page 115. In a large heavy kettle or Dutch oven melt the butter and sauté onion until golden. Add the meat and brown well on all sides. Drain off any fat. Add the wine, cover, and simmer 15 minutes. Add the boiling water, salt, and pepper. Cover and simmer 1½ to 2 hours or until meat is tender. Skim off any fat. *Serves 6 to 8.*

TO COMPLETE STEW PREPARATION WITH TOMATO SAUCE:
1 *tablespoon flour*
¼ *cup water*
1 *cup canned tomatoes*
½ *cup tomato sauce*
1 *sprig parsley, chopped*

Blend the flour and water to a paste and combine in a saucepan with tomatoes, Tomato Sauce, and parsley. Heat to boiling, and add to meat and stock. Cover and simmer 30 minutes. If Tomato Sauce is added to stew after vegetables are cooked, simmer only 15 minutes.

SPECIAL NOTES:
Tomato Sauce version: Use either red or white dry wine. Sauté vegetables in a skillet with ¼ to ½ cup vegetable oil until golden brown (except beans and peas) before adding to stew to com-

plete cooking. Firm vegetables requiring long cooking must be cooked with the meat until tender *before* the Tomato Sauce is added or they will remain hard. Soft, quick-cooking vegetables are added *after* the Tomato Sauce and cooked until just tender.

Onions—use 12 small white onions, sauté, cook tender *before* adding Tomato Sauce.

Potatoes—use 12 very small whole potatoes or cut larger ones in pieces, sauté, cook tender *before* adding Tomato Sauce.

Green Beans—cut 1½ pounds fresh beans in 3-inch lengths, do *not* sauté, cook tender *before* adding Tomato Sauce.

Green Peas—use 2 pounds tender fresh shelled peas or 2 packages frozen peas, do *not* sauté, add *after* Tomato Sauce.

Cauliflower—use 1 large head cut in 8 pieces, sprinkle with juice of ½ lemon and a little cinnamon, sauté, add *before* Tomato Sauce. Sprinkle grated cheese or lemon juice over top before serving.

Okra—use 2 pounds fresh okra, treat according to directions on page 62, sauté, add *after* Tomato Sauce.

Zucchini—use 6 to 8 very small whole zucchini or larger ones cut in pieces, sauté, add *after* Tomato Sauce. Before serving, ¼ cup grated cheese can be sprinkled over top.

Eggplant—use 2 medium-size eggplants peeled and cut in 1-inch slices, treat according to directions on page 62, sauté, add *after* Tomato Sauce. Before serving, ¼ cup grated cheese can be sprinkled over top.

TO COMPLETE STEW PREPARATION WITH AVGOLEMONO SAUCE:

Cook vegetables with meat and stock until tender. Drain the stock and measure. Add water, if necessary, to make 2 cups. Cover stew kettle to keep meat and vegetables hot. Heat the stock to boiling.

1 tablespoon flour
¼ cup water
2 cups stock

3 eggs
juice of 3 lemons

Make a paste of flour and water, add to stock, and cook for 5 minutes. In a bowl beat the eggs with electric beater until thick. Continue beating while adding, alternately in small quantities, the hot stock and lemon juice. Pour the sauce into kettle of well-drained meat and vegetables and shake pan to distribute the sauce evenly. Do not cover or reheat or it will curdle. Serve immediately.

SPECIAL NOTES:
Avgolemono Sauce version: Use only dry white wine. Do *not* sauté vegetables before adding to stew.

Artichoke Hearts—use 2 packages frozen hearts defrosted or 2 cans of hearts well drained, place in a colander, sprinkle with juice of ½ lemon, and let stand 10 minutes before adding to meat. Cook about 10 minutes.

Celery—use 1 large or 2 small heads stripped of tough outer stalks and cut in 2-inch pieces, leaves and all. Cook about 20 minutes or until tender.

Endive—use 6 to 8 whole endive, cook about 20 minutes.

Dandelion Greens—use only early spring dandelions, cook about 20 minutes.

PILAFFI TAS KEBAB

[Meat with Tomato Sauce over Rice]

This version of pilaf combines meat with sauce and rice which has been boiled separately. Follow the directions for Basic Stew on page 136, using the Tomato Sauce version. Prepare boiled rice, toss it with a little melted butter and place in a deep serving bowl with a well in the center for the meat. Pour the sauce over it.

ATZEM PILAFFI

[Lamb Pilaf with Tomato]

This is the Greek version of an ancient Turkish dish.

3 pounds lamb shoulder, cut into serving pieces
1 tablespoon butter
2 onions, chopped
salt and pepper
½ cup dry wine
4 cups boiling water
1 cup canned tomatoes
½ cup tomato sauce
¼ teaspoon cinnamon
1 tablespoon flour (in paste)
1 cup rice
2 tablespoons butter

Treat the meat according to directions on page 115. Season the meat with salt and pepper. Melt the butter in a large heavy kettle, add meat and onion and brown well. Add the wine, cover, and simmer 10 minutes. Add 2 cups boiling water, cover, and simmer 2 hours or until meat is tender. Skim off the fat.

In a saucepan combine and heat the tomatoes, tomato sauce, cinnamon, and flour paste. Add to meat and cook about 10 minutes. Add remaining 2 cups boiling water to meat, bring to boil again, and add rice. Cover and cook 18 minutes. In a small pan brown the butter and pour over the lamb and rice. This is good served with either yogurt or with feta cheese on top. *Serves 6.*

STEFADO

[Beef Braised with Onion]

This is a very popular winter dish. Served with boiled cauliflower, crusty hard bread, and retsina wine, it makes a typical Greek meal.

3 pounds beef chuck
salt and pepper
1 tablespoon butter or olive oil
1 onion, chopped
3 cloves of garlic, finely chopped
4 tablespoons dry red wine
4 cups boiling water
1 tablespoon whole mixed spice
3 pounds small white onions

SAUCE:
1 tablespoon flour
¼ cup water
1 cup canned tomatoes
½ cup tomato sauce
1 teaspoon salt
¼ teaspoon pepper
4 bay leaves
⅓ cup wine vinegar
½ cup dry red wine

Wash the meat, cut into serving pieces, sprinkle with salt and pepper, and set aside. In a heavy kettle or Dutch oven heat the butter or oil and sauté the onion and garlic until golden brown. Add the meat and brown on all sides. Add the wine and the boiling water. Insert the spice in a cheesecloth bag, tie closed, and add. Cover and simmer for 2 to 3 hours.

Peel the onions, leave them whole, and steam them with a little water in a saucepan until cooked through.

In another saucepan combine the ingredients for the sauce, first making a paste of the flour and water. Cook for 10 minutes, stirring occasionally.

Skim the fat from the meat kettle. Add the onions, then the sauce, and stir gently so as not to break the onions. Cover tightly and cook for 30 minutes without removing the lid. Remove the spice bag before serving. *Serves 6.*

VODINO ME KASTANA

[Beef with Chestnuts]

This dish comes from northern Greece.

3 pounds beef chuck
salt and pepper
cold water to cover
2 pounds chestnuts
1 onion, grated
1 cup boiling water (if no remaining stock)
1 tablespoon sugar
4 slices bread
2 tablespoons butter

Cut the beef into 2-inch cubes and sprinkle with salt and pepper. Put in a large heavy kettle and cover the meat with cold water. Cover tightly and cook over a medium flame for 1 to 1½ hours or until meat is tender.

Slash the shells of the chestnuts, place in a baking pan, and roast in the oven at 400 degrees for 15 minutes. When cool peel the shells and skins from the chestnuts, being careful not to break them. Set them aside.

When the meat is tender, remove from the kettle with any remaining liquid. Remove all but 2 tablespoons of the fat from the kettle. Sauté the onion in this. Add the meat and chestnuts and 1 cup of liquid—remaining stock if any, or boiling water.

In a small pan caramelize the sugar with 1 teaspoon hot water. When it is a rich brown color add to the meat. Cover and cook for 40 minutes.

Cut bread in squares for croutons and brown in butter. Arrange them on a platter and cover with meat and chestnuts. *Serves 6.*

KREAS KRASSATO

[Steak in Wine]

2 pounds top round steak
salt and pepper
3 tablespoons butter
1½ cups dry red wine
Lemon wedges (for garnish)

Pound the steak and season with salt and pepper. Melt the butter in a large heavy skillet. Brown the meat well on both sides. Pour the wine over the steak, cover tightly, and simmer for 1 hour. Serve with wedges of lemon on the side. *Serves 4.*

ARNI KRASSATO

[Lamb Braised in Wine]

1 three-pound boned and rolled lamb shoulder
salt and pepper
2 tablespoons butter
2½ cups dry red wine

Sprinkle salt and pepper over the lamb. In a heavy kettle or Dutch oven melt the butter, add lamb, and brown well on all sides. Add 1 cup wine, cover tightly, and simmer for 1 hour. Skim off the fat. Heat 1 cup wine, add to the meat, and cook 1 more hour. Skim off fat again. Heat and pour in the last ½ cup of wine and cook ½ hour longer. If meat is not done add about ¼ cup more wine and continue cooking until tender. There should be a little sauce in the pan to serve with meat. *Serves 4 to 6.*

ARNI BREEZOLES ME SALTSA

[Lamb Chops in Sauce]

4 large thick shoulder lamb chops
salt and pepper
flour for coating
3 tablespoons butter

SAUCE:
½ cup tomato sauce
½ cup dry white wine
1 cup water
¼ teaspoon wine vinegar
½ teaspoon capers
¼ teaspoon dry mustard
½ teaspoon salt
dash of pepper
½ cup small whole mushrooms, fresh or canned

Season the chops with salt and pepper and coat with flour. Melt the butter in a heavy skillet and brown the chops. Remove to a plate and use the same skillet to make the sauce. Combine all ingredients with drippings in skillet and cook for 10 minutes. Skim off any fat and return the chops to skillet. Cover and simmer for 1 hour. *Serves 4.*

ZAKINTHOU BREEZOLES

[Smothered Chops, Ionian Style]

This recipe for either lamb or veal chops comes from Zakintho in the Ionian Islands.

4 *large thick chops*
salt and pepper
2 *tablespoons flour for coating*
¼ *cup vegetable oil*
3 *cloves garlic, finely chopped (more or less to taste)*
¼ *cup chopped parsley*
1 *cup canned tomatoes*
½ *cup tomato sauce*
3 *tablespoons wine vinegar*
¼ *cup dry white wine*

Season the chops with salt and pepper. Pound the flour into the meat. Heat vegetable oil in a medium-size skillet and brown the chops on both sides. Combine the garlic and parsley in a small dish. In a bowl blend together the tomatoes, tomato sauce, vinegar, and wine. Spread half the garlic and parsley over two chops in skillet. Spoon a few tablespoons of the tomato mixture over them. Pile remaining two chops on top, spread with balance of garlic and parsley, and pour remaining tomato mixture over them. Cover tightly and simmer for 1 hour. *Serves 4.*

VEDELO KRASSATO

[Veal Rolls with Bacon in Wine]

1½ *pounds veal cutlet*
3 *tablespoons butter*
salt and pepper
8 *strips bacon*
1 *cup dry red wine*
2 *teaspoons flour*
1 *cup water*

Pound veal cutlet thin and cut into four pieces. Melt butter in a skillet and brush a little over meat. Salt and pepper each piece of meat. Fold each piece over into a roll and tie ends with a string to hold roll together. Wrap 2 strips of bacon around each piece and hold in place with small skewers. Fry the veal rolls in butter, turning to brown all sides. Remove all fat from pan. Warm the wine and add to pan. Cover and simmer 30 minutes or until wine is absorbed. Skim off any fat. With a little of the water make a paste of flour, add to water, and bring to a boil. Add this to veal, cover, and cook over a low flame for 1 hour. Skim off any fat before serving. *Serves 4.*

SOUTZOUKAKIA SMYRNEIKA

[Meat Rolls in Sauce]

MEAT ROLLS:

1 pound ground chuck beef
½ pound lean ground pork
1 large onion, grated
2 tablespoons chopped parsley
1 clove garlic, finely chopped
2 teaspoons salt
¼ teaspoon pepper
¼ teaspoon cumin
2 bay leaves, crushed
2 eggs
flour for coating
½ cup vegetable oil

SAUCE:

2 tablespoons butter
1 cup tomato sauce
1 teaspoon salt
¼ teaspoon sugar
½ cup dry red wine
1½ cups water

Mix together in a bowl the meat, onion, parsley, seasonings, and eggs. Shape like small sausages and roll in flour. Heat the oil in a heavy skillet and brown the meat rolls well. Drain on paper towels. Drain all fat from skillet. Combine all ingredients for the sauce in the skillet. Bring to a boil and add the meat rolls. Cover, reduce heat, and simmer 30 minutes. *Serves 4 to 6.*

KREAS SALTSA

[Meat Sauce for Spaghetti]

2 *tablespoons butter*
1 *large onion, chopped*
1 *clove garlic, chopped*
1 *small green pepper, seeded and chopped*
1 *pound lean ground chuck beef*
½ *pound lean ground pork*
2 *teaspoons salt*
¼ *teaspoon pepper*
¼ *teaspoon cinnamon*
2 *bay leaves, crushed*
½ *cup dry red wine*
1 *cup canned tomatoes*
2 *cups tomato sauce*
½ *cup hot water*
½ *cup grated kefalotyri cheese plus 1 cup for topping (or*
   Parmesan or Romano)

Melt the butter in a heavy skillet and sauté the onion, garlic, and green pepper. Add the meat and brown well. Add the seasonings and wine, cover, and simmer 15 minutes. Add the tomatoes, tomato sauce, and water. Cover and simmer 1 hour. Remove from flame, add the cheese, and mix well. *Serves 8.*

Serve the meat sauce over cooked thin spaghetti arranging on platter in layers as follows:

3 tablespoons cheese over bottom of platter
½ cooked spaghetti
2 tablespoons grated cheese
½ meat sauce
balance of spaghetti
2 tablespoons cheese
balance of meat sauce
balance of cheese

DOLMADES

[Meat Wrapped in Grape Leaves]

These are made in many Middle Eastern countries, but only in Greece are they served with Avgolemono Sauce. Grape leaves are available in jars in specialty food shops.

STOCK:
2 pounds lamb shoulder, cubed
1 tablespoon butter
1 onion, chopped
¼ cup dry white wine
4 cups boiling water

DOLMADES:
30 grape leaves (1 small jar)
1½ pounds lean ground chuck beef
1 tablespoon salt
¼ teaspoon pepper
1 tablespoon crushed dry mint leaves

1 small onion, grated
2 eggs
½ teaspoon baking soda
2 tablespoons dry white wine
⅓ cup rice

SAUCE:

3 cups stock
2 teaspoons flour
2 teaspoons water
3 eggs
juice of 3 small lemons

Treat the meat according to directions on page 115. In a large heavy kettle or Dutch oven melt the butter and sauté meat and chopped onion until well browned. Add the wine, cover, and simmer 10 minutes. Add the boiling water, cover, and cook for 2 hours. Skim off the fat.

Rinse the grape leaves in cold water three times to remove brine preservative. Drop into a pan of boiling water and soak for 1 hour to soften.

To make dolmades, combine all ingredients, combining first the soda and wine and adding this to the mixture last. Mix together well and form into 30 small balls. Drain the leaves. Wrap each meat ball in a grape leaf, folding in the sides to seal (see detailed instructions for wrapping on pages 25–26).

Measure the meat stock and add water if necessary to make 6 cups. Remove bones from meat and leave meat in bottom of kettle. Arrange the dolmades in layers over the meat. Place a heavy plate over them inside the kettle to keep them from unrolling. Return the meat stock to the kettle. It will come above the level of the plate. Cover the kettle and cook over a medium flame for 30 minutes.

Remove the stock and keep the pan of dolmades covered and

hot over a very low flame. Measure the stock and add water if necessary to make 3 cups. Make a paste of the flour and water, combine with stock in a saucepan, and simmer gently 5 minutes. Using an electric beater, beat the eggs in a large bowl until very thick. By the spoonful gradually add the hot stock and lemon juice alternately while continuing to beat. Pour the sauce over the hot dolmades and shake the pan to distribute the sauce evenly. Serve immediately and do not stir, cover, or reheat. *Serves 6.*

LAHANIKA YEMISTA ME ARNI

[Vegetables Stuffed with Lamb]

STOCK:
3 pounds lamb shanks, each cut in half
2 tablespoons butter
2 onions, minced
2 teaspoons salt
½ teaspoon pepper
4 cups boiling water

VEGETABLES:
2 very small eggplants
2 small zucchini
2 small green peppers
2 firm tomatoes

MEAT STUFFING:
1 pound ground lamb
1 small onion, grated
1 teaspoon salt
¼ teaspoon pepper
1 teaspoon chopped parsley

1 egg
½ cup rice
¼ cup dry white wine
boiling water
Avgolemono Sauce (page 136) or yogurt served on side

Treat the lamb shanks according to directions on page 115.
In a large heavy kettle or Dutch oven melt the butter and sauté
the onions until golden. Add the meat and brown well. Add salt,
pepper, and boiling water, cover, and simmer 2 hours. Skim off
fat. Remove bones and discard.

Cut eggplants in half lengthwise. Scoop out centers but leave
unpeeled. Treat according to directions on page 62. Pare and
scoop out centers of other vegetables.

Combine all the ingredients for the meat stuffing. Stuff the
prepared vegetables and place them in the kettle with cooked
meat and stock. If there is extra meat stuffing make into meat balls
and add also. Pour in the wine and enough boiling water to half
cover vegetables. Cover and cook 40 minutes or until rice is
thoroughly cooked. If this is to be served with Avgolemono Sauce,
drain stock and use for sauce following directions with Basic
Stew on page 136. *Serves 6 to 8.*

HIRINO ME LAHANO

[Pork with Cabbage]

This dish is served only in winter.

2 pounds pork butt
salt and pepper
1 tablespoon vegetable oil
1 onion, sliced
½ cup dry red wine
3 cups boiling water

1 head cabbage (about 2 pounds)
1 tablespoon flour
½ cup water
1 cup canned tomatoes
1 teaspoon salt
lemon wedges (for garnish)

Cut pork into 2-inch cubes, removing as much fat as possible. Sprinkle with salt and pepper. Heat the oil in a large kettle. Brown the onion and meat, then drain off the fat. Add the wine, cover, and simmer 15 minutes. Add the boiling water, cover, and cook over a low flame for 2 hours. Skim off any fat.

Wash the cabbage and cut in 8 wedges. Add to the meat and cook 15 minutes. Make a paste of the flour and water and combine it in a saucepan with tomatoes and salt. Heat to boiling, then add to the meat and cabbage. Continue cooking 30 minutes or until cabbage is tender. Serve with lemon wedges on the side. *Serves 6.*

KOUNELI STEFADO

[Rabbit Stew]

1 rabbit (about 2½ pounds)
1 cup plus 3 tablespoons wine vinegar
salt and pepper
flour for coating plus 2 tablespoons with little water in paste
¾ cup olive oil
2 cups dry white wine
16 very small whole white onions
2 cloves garlic
1 cup tomato sauce
3 bay leaves
½ teaspoon rosemary leaves

Clean and wash the rabbit and cut into serving pieces. Place in a large bowl, sprinkle with salt, and pour ½ cup vinegar over it. Add enough water to cover and let stand several hours. Wash and dry the rabbit, sprinkle with salt and pepper, and dredge with flour. Heat the olive oil in a skillet and fry the rabbit until light brown on all sides. Transfer to a large heavy kettle or Dutch oven, pour half the wine over it, cover tightly, and steam for 15 minutes. Fry the onions in the skillet until light brown and add, along with garlic, to the rabbit. In the same skillet combine the tomato sauce, balance of wine, more salt and pepper, bay leaves, rosemary, balance of vinegar, and flour paste. Cook together for 10 minutes, then add to rabbit. Cover and simmer until rabbit is tender. *Serves 4.*

KOUNELI ME SKORDALIA

[Rabbit with Garlic Sauce]

1 small rabbit (about 2½ pounds)
1 cup wine vinegar
salt and pepper
½ cup olive oil
½ cup dry white wine
½ cup Skordalia (garlic sauce), pages 238, 239.

Clean and wash the rabbit and cut into serving pieces. Place in a large bowl, sprinkle with salt, and pour vinegar over it. Cover with cold water and allow to stand for several hours. Wash and dry the rabbit and sprinkle with salt and pepper. Heat the oil in a heavy skillet, add the rabbit, and fry slowly until golden brown on all sides. Add the wine, cover, and cook until rabbit is tender. Prepare Skordalia and spread over the rabbit before serving. *Serves 4.*

BREADS

VASILOPITA I *[New Year's Bread]*

VASILOPITA II *[New Year's Sweet Bread]*

PASCHALINE KOULOURA *[Easter Bread Ring]*

TSOUREKE *[Easter Twist]*

CHRISTOPSOMO *[Christmas Bread]*

PSOME *[Greek City Bread]*

PSOMAKIA *[Sesame Seed Rolls]*

KOULOURAKIA *[Sweet Bread Rings]*

BOBOTA *[Village Corn Bread]*

PAXIMADE I *[Greek Toast]*

PAXIMADE II *[Greek Toast, Lenten Version]*

11 · Breads

BREAD IS by far the most widely consumed food in Greece. It accompanies every meal and is the mainstay of a poor villager's diet. Breads are important among holiday foods too, especially for Christmas, New Year's, and Easter.

Three kinds of bread are available in the cities for everyday use, all made of white flour. The standard loaf, round and usually topped with sesame seeds, is called simply psome (bread). Kouloura is a ring loaf with an open center which is made of richer dough. A special version of this is made for Easter bread. Another bread which is always available is Frantzola, a long loaf like French bread. There are also individual rolls which usually have sesame seed topping and Koulourakia, hard ring rolls made in great quantity commercially and sold by street vendors.

Village bread lacks both the variety and quality of city bread. It is made, of course, of dark flour as white flour is in limited supply and more expensive than most villagers can afford. Villagers grow their own grain and grind it into flour in community

mills. If the wheat grain supply is short, barley grain is blended
with the wheat. Wherever grain crops cannot be grown, cornmeal
is substituted for wheat flour in breadmaking.

VASILOPITA 1

[New Year's Bread]

The ceremonious cutting of this bread is described in Chapter
2, page 7.

BREAD:

1 cup milk
2 yeast cakes
¾ cup sugar plus 2 teaspoons
1 teaspoon salt
⅓ cup melted butter
3 eggs, well beaten
1 teaspoon grated lemon rind
½ teaspoon crushed masteha*
1 teaspoon crushed mahlepe*
⅓ cup lukewarm water
6 cups sifted all-purpose flour
1 or 2 clean coins

TOPPING:

3 tablespoons light cream
½ teaspoon sugar
¼ teaspoon cinnamon
½ cup sesame seeds

*Masteha and mahlepe are Greek flavorings which give this bread its
distinct character. They are expensive and difficult to obtain and may be
omitted.

Scald the milk and set aside to cool. Crumble the yeast in a small bowl, sprinkle with 2 teaspoons sugar, and set aside for 10 minutes. When milk is cool combine it with remaining sugar, salt, melted butter, beaten eggs, lemon rind, masteha, and mahlepe in a large bowl. Beat with electric beater for 5 minutes. Add the lukewarm water to the yeast, blend until smooth, then stir into the mixture. Add the flour and knead the dough until soft and pliable. Place on a floured board and continue kneading for 10 minutes. Thoroughly grease the sides and bottom of a large bowl. Turn the dough into it and rotate until all sides are greased. Cover with a heavy cloth and put in a warm place to rise for two hours.

After two hours, turn the dough out on a floured board and knead lightly. Divide into two parts and put a clean coin in the center of each, or for one loaf leave dough in one piece and use one coin. Then knead until the coins are well hidden. Shape the dough to fit into two greased 9-inch round cake pans or one 12-inch round pan.

Combine the cream, sugar, and cinnamon. Brush over the tops of loaves and sprinkle with sesame seeds. Cover with a cloth and put in a warm place to rise for two hours. Bake at 350 degrees for 50 minutes for 9-inch loaves and 1 hour for 12-inch loaf. Remove from pan immediately and cool. *Makes two 9-inch round loaves or one 12-inch round loaf.*

VASILOPITA II

[New Year's Sweet Bread]

This cake-like bread never has a coin baked in it. This is a version made by Greeks from Smyrna.

3 eggs, separated
¾ cup sugar

3 tablespoons soft butter
½ cup orange juice
1 teaspoon grated orange rind
3 tablespoons brandy
2 cups sifted cake flour
½ teaspoon salt
2 teaspoons baking powder
¼ teaspoon baking soda
powdered sugar (for topping)

Beat the egg yolks for 5 minutes with an electric beater, slowly adding the sugar. When thick, add the soft butter and beat 3 minutes longer. Add half the orange juice, the rind, 1 tablespoon brandy, and mix together with a large spoon. Beat the egg whites until stiff, then fold half of the beaten whites into the first mixture. Sift together the flour, salt, and baking powder. In small amounts add half the sifted ingredients to the mixture, mixing well after each addition. Dissolve the baking soda in 1 tablespoon of the brandy and add. Add remaining orange juice, brandy, and flour, and mix well. Fold in the remaining egg whites. Pour the batter into a well-greased 9-inch round cake pan and bake at 350 degrees for 35 minutes. Remove from pan immediately. Place on a cake plate and sprinkle top with powdered sugar. This bread is best when served warm. *Makes one 9-inch round loaf.*

PASCHALINE KOULOURA

[Easter Bread Ring]

To a Greek, Easter would not be complete without this on the table.

BREAD:
2 yeast cakes
½ cup sugar plus 2 teaspoons

1 cup milk
1 teaspoon salt
⅓ cup melted butter
2 eggs, well beaten
¼ cup orange juice
¼ cup lukewarm water
6 cups sifted all-purpose flour

TOPPING:
2 tablespoons light cream
1 teaspoon sugar
½ teaspoon cinnamon
½ cup sesame seeds
1 uncooked egg, dyed red

Crumble the yeast cakes in a small bowl, sprinkle with 2 teaspoons sugar, and set aside for 10 minutes. Scald the milk, cool it, then pour into a large bowl. Add the ½ cup sugar, salt, butter, eggs, and orange juice. Beat with a rotary beater for 5 minutes. Dissolve the yeast in the lukewarm water and add. Add the flour and knead until the dough is smooth. Turn out on a floured board and continue to knead a few minutes longer. Grease the bowl and return the dough, turning to grease all sides. Cover with a cloth and put in a warm place to rise for 2 hours. The dough should double in bulk.

Turn the dough out on a floured board. Cut off two pieces to roll into two 12-inch-long strips 2 inches wide. Shape the remaining dough in a circle to fit a greased 12-inch round pan. Place the strips across the bread in the shape of a cross.

Combine the cream, sugar, and cinnamon and brush over top. Sprinkle with sesame seeds and place the red egg in the center of the cross, pressing in firmly. Cover with a cloth and put in a warm place to rise for 2 hours. About 10 minutes before baking, press the egg down gently. Bake at 350 degrees for 1 hour. *Makes one 12-inch loaf.*

TSOUREKE

[Easter Twist]

This bread is richer than Kouloura and does not have the red
egg on top. The recipe originated with Greeks of Smyrna.

BREAD:

2 *yeast cakes*
1 *cup lukewarm water*
1 *cup milk*
1¼ *cups sugar*
1 *teaspoon salt*
5 *cups sifted all-purpose flour*
¾ *cup butter*
3 *eggs, well beaten*
¼ *cup orange juice*
½ *cup white raisins*

TOPPING:

¼ *cup light cream*
¼ *teaspoon sugar*
½ *cup ground blanched almonds*

Dissolve the yeast in lukewarm water. Scald the milk and cool
to lukewarm. Combine the yeast, milk, 1 teaspoon sugar, and salt
in a large bowl. Add 2 cups of the flour and mix thoroughly.
Cover the bowl with a cloth and put in a warm place to rise for
2 hours.

In another bowl cream the butter and remaining sugar. Add
the beaten eggs, orange juice, and raisins and mix thoroughly.
Add the risen dough and blend together well, then add remaining flour and knead into the dough. Turn out on a floured board
and knead for 10 minutes to make smooth and pliable. Place in

a well-greased warm bowl, rotating to grease all sides. Cover with a cloth and put in a warm place to rise for 1½ hours, when the dough should double in bulk.

Turn the dough out on a floured board and knead lightly. Grease a 12-inch round pan. Cut the dough into 3 pieces and roll each until long enough to braid into a round twist to fit pan. Combine the cream and sugar, and brush on top. Sprinkle with ground almonds. Cover and put in a warm place to rise for 1½ hours, then bake at 350 degrees for 1 hour. *Makes one 12-inch round loaf.*

CHRISTOPSOMO
[Christmas Bread]

This holiday bread is served as a sweet, never with butter, but sometimes with honey.

BREAD:

1 cup milk
2 yeast cakes
¾ cup sugar plus 2 teaspoons
½ cup melted butter
3 eggs
1 teaspoon salt
1 cup lukewarm water
*1 teaspoon crushed masteha**
½ cup white raisins
½ cup chopped canned figs, well drained
½ cup chopped walnuts
6 cups sifted all-purpose flour

* Masteha is a Greek flavoring which gives this bread a unique and lingering flavor. It is expensive and difficult to obtain and may be omitted.

TOPPING:

¼ cup corn syrup
¼ cup honey
juice of ½ orange
blanched almonds

Scald the milk and set aside to cool. Crumble the yeast cakes in a small bowl, sprinkle with 2 teaspoons sugar, and let stand for 10 minutes.

In a large bowl combine the cooled milk, remaining sugar, butter, eggs, and salt. Beat with a rotary beater. Dissolve the yeast in the lukewarm water and add. Add the masteha, raisins, figs, walnuts, and flour, mixing thoroughly by hand. Turn the dough out on a floured board and knead for 10 minutes. The dough should be smooth but loose. Place the dough in a buttered warm bowl, turning to butter all sides. Cover with a cloth and put in a warm place to rise for 2 hours. It should double in bulk.

Turn the dough out on a floured board, knead a little, and divide into 2 pieces. Shape each to fit a greased 9-inch round cake pan. Combine the corn syrup, honey, and orange juice in a small saucepan and boil gently for 10 minutes. Brush this glaze over the loaves and decorate the tops with blanched almonds. Cover the loaves with a cloth and put in a warm place to rise for 1½ to 2 hours. Bake at 325 degrees for 1 hour. After 20 minutes cover with aluminum foil to prevent nuts from getting too dry. *Makes two 9-inch round cakes or one 12-inch round cake.*

PSOME

[Greek City Bread]

BREAD:

1 cup milk
3 tablespoons sugar
1 tablespoon salt

¼ *cup melted margarine*
1 *egg, slightly beaten*
2 *yeast cakes*
1 *cup lukewarm water*
6 *cups sifted all-purpose flour*

TOPPING:
2 *tablespoons light cream*
4 *tablespoons sesame seeds*

Scald the milk and let it cool to lukewarm. In a large bowl combine the sugar, salt, margarine, and egg. Stir in the cooled milk. Dissolve the yeast cakes in the lukewarm water and add, then add the sifted flour and mix together well. Turn the dough out on a floured board and knead until very smooth. Grease a large warm bowl, transfer the dough to the bowl, and rotate to grease all sides. Cover with a cloth and put in a warm place to rise for 1½ to 2 hours or until double in bulk.

Turn the dough out on a floured board and knead a few minutes. Divide into 2 pieces and fit each into a well-greased 9-inch round cake pan. Brush each loaf with cream and sprinkle with sesame seeds. Cover and put in a warm place to rise for 2 hours. Bake at 350 degrees for 40 minutes. *Makes two 9-inch round loaves.*

PSOMAKIA

[Sesame Seed Rolls]

ROLLS:
2 *yeast cakes*
5 *tablespoons sugar*
1 *cup milk*
⅓ *cup melted butter*
1 *teaspoon salt*

2 *eggs, well beaten*
2 *tablespoons orange juice*
1 *teaspoon grated orange rind*
1 *cup lukewarm water*
6 *cups sifted all-purpose flour*

TOPPING:

¼ *cup light cream*
½ *teaspoon sugar*
1 *cup sesame seeds*

In a small bowl crumble the yeast cakes, sprinkle with 2 teaspoons of the sugar, and set aside for 10 minutes. Scald the milk and let it cool. Combine the cooled milk with the butter, remaining sugar, salt, eggs, orange juice, and orange rind and beat with electric beater for 5 minutes. Dissolve the yeast in the lukewarm water and add to the mixture, mixing thoroughly. Add the flour and mix by hand. Place the dough on a floured board and knead until smooth. Place it in a large well-greased warm bowl, turning to grease all sides. Cover with a cloth and put in a warm place to rise for 1½ to 2 hours or until double in bulk.

Turn the dough out on a floured board and knead a few times. Cut off pieces the size of a lemon, roll between palms of hands to 8 inches in length and loop into a knot. Mix the cream and sugar together and brush on knotted rolls. Dip in sesame seeds and place on a greased cookie sheet 3 inches apart. Cover with a cloth and put in a warm place to rise for 1½ hours. Bake at 350 degrees for 25 to 30 minutes. *Makes 2 dozen.*

KOULOURAKIA

[Sweet Bread Rings]

These have the same name as Easter Cookies (Chapter 12), but they are made the year round in Greece. They are sold by vendors on the street.

7 cups sifted all-purpose flour
¼ cup warm water
½ cup warm milk
2 yeast cakes
1 teaspoon salt
⅓ cup melted butter
3 eggs
⅓ cup cold milk
¾ cup sugar
1 tablespoon vanilla
2 tablespoons brandy
light cream (for brushing tops)

Sift 2 cups of the flour into a large bowl. In a small bowl combine the warm milk and water and dissolve yeast in it. Stir into
the flour and mix thoroughly. This will be a loose dough. Put in a
warm place to rise for 1½ hours.

After the first dough has risen, sift together the remaining
flour and the salt. Add the melted butter and mix until evenly
distributed. In another bowl beat the eggs slightly, add cold milk,
sugar, vanilla, and brandy, and mix together well. Add the egg
mixture to the risen dough, mixing with a heavy spoon until
smooth. Add the flour and butter mixture and knead together for
about 10 minutes until very smooth.

Cut off pieces of the dough about the size of a large walnut
and roll between the hands to a 3-inch length, then twist into a
doughnut shape and place 2 inches apart on a greased cookie
sheet. Brush tops with cream and let rise for 1½ hours. Bake at
350 degrees for 35 minutes. *Makes 4 dozen.*

BOBOTA

[Village Corn Bread]

This is a modified and more palatable version of the life-
saving sustenance for many Greeks during wartime, which was

made then only of cornmeal, honey, and water. It is not popular everywhere in Greece because many people associate it with war and poverty, but villagers have elaborated on it so many make a similar bread today.

1 cup light corn meal
1 cup sifted all-purpose flour
1 teaspoon baking powder
¼ teaspoon baking soda
½ teaspoon salt
¼ cup sugar
3 tablespoons honey
⅓ cup orange juice
¾ cup warm water
3 tablespoons vegetable oil, heated
1 teaspoon grated orange rind
½ cup currants
½ cup Basic Syrup (page 177) or powdered sugar

Sift all the dry ingredients together into a large bowl. Combine the honey, orange juice, water, and warm oil and stir into the dry mixture, beating with a large wooden spoon until smooth. Fold in the orange rind and currants. Pour the batter into a well-greased 7x7x2-inch square pan and bake at 375 degrees for 35 minutes. Leave in pan to cool, then pour ½ cup warm syrup over it or sprinkle with powdered sugar and serve immediately. *Makes 9 large or 16 small pieces.*

PAXIMADE I

[Greek Toast]

No Greek home is without this. It is served for breakfast, afternoon tea, and to children for a snack. Restaurants always have it on the table for breakfast.

2½ cups sifted all-purpose flour
2 teaspoons baking powder
½ teaspoon salt
½ cup butter
½ cup sugar
2 eggs
½ cup milk
1 teaspoon finely crushed anise seed
1 teaspoon sesame seeds

Sift together flour, baking powder, and salt. In another bowl cream the butter and sugar. Add the eggs and beat until smooth. Add the milk gradually, continuing to beat, then add anise seed. Blend in the dry ingredients, mixing until smooth. Grease a 13x4-inch loaf pan, shape the dough in the pan, and sprinkle top with sesame seeds. Bake at 350 degrees for 45 minutes. Allow to cool before removing from pan. When cold cut into thin slices and toast. Store in tins. *Makes about 40 slices.*

PAXIMADE II

[Greek Toast, Lenten Version]

This version, without butter or eggs, is served after funerals and during a period of mourning as well as during Lent.

3 cups flour
¾ cup sugar
½ teaspoon salt
¼ teaspoon finely crushed anise seed
½ cup shortening
½ cup sweet wine (muscatel preferred)
½ teaspoon baking powder
1 yeast cake

¼ cup warm water
1 teaspoon sesame seeds

Sift the flour, sugar, salt and anise seed into a bowl. Melt the shortening and blend into the dry mixture. Dissolve the baking powder in the wine and add. Dissolve the yeast in the lukewarm water and add. Mix, then knead the dough until very smooth. Grease a 13x4-inch loaf pan, shape the dough into the pan, and sprinkle the top with sesame seeds. Put in a warm place to rise for 1½ to 2 hours or until double in bulk. Bake at 350 degrees for 1 hour. Cool before removing from pan. When loaf is cold, cut into thin slices and toast. Store in tins. *Makes about 40 slices.*

DESSERTS

Basic Syrup

PASTRIES USING FILLO DOUGH:

BAKLAVA *[Honey-soaked Nut Pastry]*
GALATOBOUREKO *[Custard-filled Pastry]*
AMEGTHALA FLOYERES *[Almond-stuffed Flutes]*
KREMA FLOYERES *[Cream Flutes]*
KOPENHAYI *[Nut-filled Pastry]*
KADAIFE ROLLS

CAKES AND TORTES:

YAOURTOPITA *[Yogurt Cake]*
KARETHOPITA *[Walnut Cake]*
RAVANI I *[Sponge Almond Cake]*
RAVANI II *[Butter Almond Cake]*
COCOANUT TOURTA *[Cocoanut Cake]*
YAOURTI, KARETHOPITA ME STAFITHES *[Yogurt, Walnut, and Raisin Cake]*
PITA AYIOU FANOUREO *[St. Fanoureo's Cake]*

COOKIES AND PUFFS:

BASIC COOKIE DOUGH
PISCOTA *[Tea Cookies]*
YAOURTI PISCOTA *[Yogurt Wafers]*

COCOANUT PISCOTA [Cocoanut Drops]

SKALTSOUNAKIA [Cheese-filled Cookies]

KOURAMBIETHES [Powdered Sugar Crescent Cookies]

MELOMAKAROUNA I [Honey Mounds, Mainland Version]

MELOMAKAROUNA II [Honey Mounds, Island Version]

KOULOURAKIA [Easter Cookies]

THIPLES [Deep-fried Dainties]

SVINGOUS [Fried Sweet Puffs]

LALANGITES [Rich Sweet Puffs]

LOUKOUMADES [Lenten Sweet Puffs]

PUDDING-TYPE DESSERTS:

KASTANO FOLIA [Chestnut Nests]

HALVAH [Fried Pudding Mold]

KREMA KARAMALE [Caramel Custard]

MELI PITA [Honey Pie]

RIZOGALO [Rice Pudding]

FRUIT DESSERTS:

MEELO PITA [Apple Pie]

MEELA SVINGA [Apple Fritters]

KOUPES [Fruit Tarts]

PASTA FLORA [Fruit Squares]

VISSINO MARENGA [Sour Cherry Meringue]

TARTA STAFILIA [Fresh Grape Tart]

12 · Desserts

HONEY GLAZES, powdered sugar, nuts, and fruit toppings make Greek sweets as attractive as they are delicious. Because sweets are associated with gala occasions, they are not eaten during fast periods. Many are so rich they are preferred as a separate repast rather than the final course of a meal. Custards, bland puddings, or the sweet sun-ripened fresh fruits of the Mediterranean climate are popular for meals.

It is an act of Greek hospitality to serve guests a special treat, so every home cupboard is supplied with small pastries or cookies and liqueurs in readiness for unexpected guests. A Greek's gesture of hospitality is too ceremonious and magnanimous ever to be declined. Even in the simplest surroundings the moment becomes one of relaxed enjoyment for guest and host alike.

Many sweets were refined to their present perfection as a result of Turkish influence. For example, Loukoumades, one of the oldest known Greek sweets, evolved from unleavened wheat cakes which were fried on an iron grill, then covered with a grape-derived molasses. The use of syrup with honey as a coating was borrowed from the Turks to replace the molasses, and the cooking method changed to deep-frying to make them the sweet known today.

There are many deep-fried sweets, and they are especially popular with village cooks who find the method easier than firing up their ovens or sending food to be baked in community ovens.

Recipes using nuts call for either walnuts or almonds which are the native and very plentiful nuts of Greece. Pecans can usually be satisfactorily substituted.

Greek cakes are glazed with syrup rather than being iced with a frosting. A basic syrup combining sugar, honey, and spices is used for a dip or to pour over many pastries. The syrup can be made in quantity and stored in a cool place, though not in the refrigerator where it is apt to crystallize. The general rule for using syrup is to use it warm on cold foods and cold on warm foods. It keeps pastries moist, but syrup-soaked sweets are apt to become soggy if refrigerated.

A cookie-type dough is sometimes used for pastry shells and crusts, but pie crust as we know it is not made by the Greeks. Their flaky pastries such as Baklava are made with fillo, a special dough in sheets as thin as tissue paper which is used in many layers, each brushed with butter. Kadaife is a shredded fillo dough which is more difficult to handle than the sheets and is most successful for individual flutes made with a dry filling. It also is brushed heavily with butter before baking.

Fillo is very difficult to make successfully at home, and we recommend using the commercially prepared and packaged sheets. Sold also under the name of strudel dough, it is wrapped in 1-pound packages and is available wherever Greek or imported products are sold. Though the size of the sheets may vary according to the maker, an average package will contain 20 to 22 sheets about 17x14-inches in size. The fillo must be kept refrigerated and tightly wrapped to prevent drying out. If stored properly it can be kept in the refrigerator a month. Review the following directions before making a recipe using fillo or kadaife.

Directions for using fillo—While using fillo it is important to keep the supply covered so it retains its moisture. Unroll the package and fold the entire stack of sheets half over with the paper remaining around the top and bottom. Place a tea towel over this and remove the sheets, one at a time, from the center, always recovering immediately.

The fillo can be cut with kitchen shears to fit the pan exactly. When cut pieces are to be pieced together for a layer, use them alternating with full sheets. Use a pastry brush to spread a thin coat of melted butter over each sheet before applying the next.

Before baking a dessert made with layers of fillo, use a sharp knife to cut the panful into individual serving pieces. Each piece will then have neat edges when removed from the pan after baking. If it has a cream or other soft filling which might ooze, cut through only the upper layers. If it is a dry filling cut through all the layers right to the bottom of the pan.

Fillo is used also for the flutes and triangles made into individual pieces. For these a single sheet about 4 inches wide is used and continually folded over as the filling is wrapped inside. With each turn a dab of butter is applied. The sides must be folded over toward the center to make a seal so the filling will not leak out.

Directions for using kadaife—This is the same kind of dough as fillo but in a shredded state rather than in thin sheets. It is used for the same kinds of recipes. Because of the porous texture it must be spread a little thicker than the sheets to keep the filling sealed in. It will absorb a great deal of butter so brush the surfaces generously.

To make flutes or rolls, take a handful of the dough and spread it out on a bread board with the fingers. Brush well with butter, then place a tablespoonful of filling in the center. Roll up tightly, place on a cookie sheet, and drip melted butter over the top.

BASIC SYRUP

2 *cups sugar*
1½ *cups water*
rind of ½ lemon, finely cut
5 *whole cloves*
2 *cinnamon sticks*
1 *cup honey*
4 *tablespoons lemon juice*
2 *tablespoons rum or brandy*
1 *tablespoon rum flavoring*

In a saucepan combine sugar, water, lemon rind, cloves, and cinnamon sticks. Bring to a boil and cook until syrup thickens slightly. Remove from flame and add honey, lemon juice, liquor, and flavoring. Store in a cool place but not in refrigerator, where it is apt to crystallize. Syrup keeps well but will become strong if spices are not removed after a week. *Makes about 4 cups.*

PASTRIES USING FILLO DOUGH

BAKLAVA

[Honey-soaked Nut Pastry]

This best-known of Greek desserts is of Turkish origin. It is made in all Near Eastern countries, varied by using nuts native to the country. This version is typically Greek. See directions for using fillo on page 176.

1 *pound walnuts, coarsely chopped*
½ *pound blanched almonds, finely chopped*
½ *cup sugar*

2 teaspoons cinnamon
1½ pounds butter, melted
1 pound fillo
4 cups Basic Syrup (page 177)

Combine the chopped walnuts and almonds. Add the sugar and cinnamon and mix together thoroughly. Divide this mixture in 4 equal parts. Using a 13x9x2-inch baking pan, line the bottom with 10 layers of fillo, brushing each sheet with butter before applying the next. Sprinkle a quarter of the nut mixture over the entire layer. Add 6 more layers of fillo, brushing each layer with butter, and cover with a quarter of mixture. Repeat twice, then top with 10 layers of fillo.

Before baking, cut Baklava in 2-inch diamond-shape pieces, being sure to cut through to bottom of pan. Pour the remaining melted butter over it. Bake at 325 degrees for 1 hour, covering with aluminum foil the last 20 minutes to prevent it from getting too brown. Remove from oven and slowly pour 2 cups of cool syrup over the hot Baklava. An hour later pour the remaining 2 cups of syrup over it. Leave in the same pan and store in a cool place but not in the refrigerator. This is best served the following day but keeps well 10 days or more if properly stored. If not used within a week pour *hot* syrup over it. *Makes 40 small pieces.*

GALATOBOUREKO

[Custard-filled Pastry]

This is especially popular after Easter, using the plentiful supply of eggs and milk. It requires a thicker syrup than the Basic Syrup. See directions for handling fillo on page 176.

½ cup farina
¼ cup cornstarch

1 *teaspoon salt*
6 *cups milk*
6 *eggs*
¾ *cup sugar*
1 *teaspoon vanilla*
½ *pound fillo*
½ *pound butter, melted*

SYRUP:
2 *cups sugar*
1½ *cups water*
1 *cinnamon stick*
2 *whole cloves*
¼ *lemon—juice and pieces of rind*

Combine farina, cornstarch, and salt in a large saucepan. Add the milk and cook over a low flame, stirring constantly, until mixture thickens. Remove from flame and cool.

Separate 3 of the eggs and beat the whites until very stiff. In another bowl beat the remaining whole eggs and the 3 yolks until thick. Add the sugar and vanilla and mix thoroughly. After the milk has cooled slowly add it to the egg mixture, blending well. Fold in the beaten egg whites.

Use half the fillo sheets arranged in layers, each brushed with butter, to line a 13x9x2-inch pan. Pour the filling over fillo and cover with remaining sheets of fillo, each brushed with butter. Pour any remaining butter over the top. Score through the top layers of fillo in diamond-shape pieces. Bake at 325 degrees for 1 hour.

Combine the ingredients for syrup in a saucepan and boil until the syrup spins a thread from a spoon. After Galatoboureko has cooled pour warm syrup over it. It is best when served 6 to 8 hours after baking. It is apt to become soggy if refrigerated. *Makes 20 pieces.*

AMEGTHALA FLOYERES

[Almond-stuffed Flutes]

These are shaped to imitate the reed flutes of the shepherds.
See directions for handling fillo on page 176.

3 eggs
½ cup sugar
1 teaspoon cinnamon
1 cup ground blanched almonds
3 tablespoons light cream
12 sheets fillo
½ pound butter, melted
syrup (see Galatoboureko, page 178)

Beat the eggs with an electric beater until very thick. Combine
the sugar, cinnamon, and almonds and fold into the eggs. Fold in
the cream.

Cut the fillo lengthwise in strips 4 inches wide. Arrange in
a stack and cover well. Remove one at a time to make the flutes.
Brush butter over entire length of a fillo strip. Place 1 tablespoon
of filling 2 inches from bottom in center of strip. Fold over once
to cover the filling, then fold each edge over ½ inch toward center
to seal ends and prevent filling from leaking out. Roll over con-
tinuously and tightly to end of fillo and place roll on a cookie
sheet. Brush with remaining butter.

Bake the flutes at 350 degrees about 20 minutes until golden
brown. Remove from oven and transfer immediately to a deep
pan, arranging close together in rows. After they have cooled
pour warm syrup over them. Flutes must be stored with their
syrup, but do not refrigerate. These will keep well for several
days. *Makes about 48.*

KREMA FLOYERES
[Cream Flutes]

4 *teaspoons cornstarch*
¼ *cup water*
2 *cups milk*
¼ *cup farina*
¼ *cup sugar*
¼ *teaspoon salt*
1 *tablespoon vanilla*
¼ *teaspoon cinnamon*
2 *eggs plus 2 yolks*
12 *sheets fillo*
½ *pound butter, melted*
syrup (see Galatoboureko, page 178)

Dissolve the cornstarch in the water and combine in a large saucepan with the milk, farina, sugar, and salt. Cook over a low flame, stirring constantly, until mixture thickens to consistency of a heavy white sauce. Remove from flame and add vanilla and cinnamon. Beat the eggs well, then stir into the hot mixture, mixing well.

Using fillo strips 4 inches wide, make the flutes according to directions given for Almond Flutes, above. Bake at 350 degrees for 20 minutes. Remove from oven and transfer immediately to a deep pan, arranging close together in rows. Cool slightly, then pour warm syrup over them. Serve these the day they are made as they become soggy by the next day. *Makes about 48.*

KOPENHAYI

[Nut-filled Pastry]

This is a rich nut-filled pastry a little like Baklava but with a sweet-dough bottom crust and fillo pastry on top. It is best if served within three days. See directions for handling fillo, page 176.

PASTRY DOUGH:
½ cup soft butter
¾ cup sugar
1 egg
2 tablespoons brandy
1 teaspoon vanilla
2½ cups sifted cake flour
1 teaspoon baking powder
¼ teaspoon salt

FILLING:
10 eggs
½ cup sugar
1 cup ground almonds
1 cup ground walnuts
¼ cup crushed zweiback
½ teaspoon cinnamon
2 tablespoons light cream
1 tablespoon vanilla
½ pound fillo
½ pound butter, melted
4 cups Basic Syrup (page 177)

Cream butter and sugar, add egg, brandy, and vanilla, and beat until smooth. Sift together the dry ingredients and fold into mixture. Knead until thoroughly blended and smooth. Press evenly over the bottom of a 13x9x2-inch baking pan. Bake at 350 degrees for 15 minutes.

To make the filling, beat the eggs with an electric beater until very thick. Combine the sugar, nuts, zweiback, and cinnamon, and fold into the beaten eggs. Fold in the cream and vanilla, mixing well. Pour this over the baked pastry crust. Cover with fillo sheets, brushing each with melted butter. Pour any remaining butter evenly over the top. Score through the fillo in diamond shapes for size pieces desired. Bake at 325 degrees for 45 minutes. While warm pour cool syrup over it. Serve the following day. *Makes about 20 pieces.*

KADAIFE ROLLS

See directions for handling kadaife on page 176.

2 *eggs*
¼ *cup sugar*
2 *cups ground walnuts*
1 *tablespoon cinnamon*
2 *teaspoons light cream*
1 *pound kadaife*
¾ *pound butter, melted*
2½ *cups Basic Syrup (page 177)*

Beat the eggs until thick, gradually adding the sugar. Add the walnuts, cinnamon, and cream, and mix well. Using a small handful of kadaife dough for each roll, follow directions on page 176. Place the rolls on a cookie sheet and pour remaining butter over them. Bake at 350 degrees 50 minutes to 1 hour until golden brown. Transfer to a plate, arranging close together. Pour syrup over them and let stand until the following day before serving. *Makes 24.*

CAKES AND TORTES

YAOURTOPITA

[Yogurt Cake]

This is very popular with American friends. The recipe came from the Queen's Homemaking School at Karetena in the Peloponnesus.

¾ cup soft butter
1½ cups sugar
1 teaspoon grated lemon rind
6 eggs, separated
1¾ cups yogurt
½ cup chopped blanched almonds
1 teaspoon vanilla
½ teaspoon baking soda
¼ cup cognac or rum
2 cups sifted cake flour
2 teaspoons baking powder
½ teaspoon salt
½ teaspoon almond flavoring
1½ cups Basic Syrup (page 177)

Cream together the butter, sugar, and lemon rind with an electric beater. Add the egg yolks and mix well, then add the yogurt and beat for one minute. Add the almonds and vanilla and blend well. Dissolve the baking soda in the liquor and add, then beat for one minute. Sift together twice the flour, baking powder, and salt, gradually add to the mixture, and beat for two minutes. Beat the egg whites until stiff, toward the end adding the almond flavoring. Gently fold them into the batter. Pour into a greased 10-inch tube pan and bake at 325 degrees for 35 minutes. Remove from pan to a large cake plate and allow to cool. When cool pour the warm syrup over it slowly, ½ cup at a time, at 15 minute intervals so the cake can absorb it. Allow to stand for several hours before serving. Will keep a week at room temperature if tightly covered. *Serves 16.*

KARETHOPITA

[Walnut Cake]

There are many variations to this, for it is made in all parts of Greece using the plentiful supply of walnuts. It is a heavy dessert favored during winter.

3 tablespoons soft butter
1½ cups sugar
1 tablespoon grated orange rind
12 eggs, separated
2 tablespoons brandy
½ cup water
1 cup ground zweiback
2 teaspoons baking powder
½ teaspoon salt
1 teaspoon ground cinnamon
½ teaspoon ground cloves
2 cups ground walnuts
½ cup coarsely chopped walnuts (for topping)
1 to 1½ cups Basic Syrup (page 177)

Cream together the butter, sugar, and orange rind with an electric beater. Add the egg yolks and beat until fluffy. Add the brandy and water and mix well. Combine all the dry ingredients and add, blending well. Beat the egg whites until stiff and fold into the mixture. Pour into a greased 8x12x3-inch pan and sprinkle the coarsely chopped nuts over top. Bake at 350 degrees for 35 to 40 minutes. Top should be golden brown. Allow to cool in pan, then cut into diamond-shape pieces. Pour warm syrup over the top. This is best served the following day but will keep well a week at room temperature if tightly covered. Do not refrigerate. *Makes 25 to 30 small pieces.*

RAVANI I

[Sponge Almond Cake]

10 eggs, separated
2 cups powdered sugar
¾ cup finely crushed zweiback
¾ cup finely chopped blanched almonds
½ teaspoon baking powder
½ teaspoon cream of tartar
1 teaspoon ground orange rind
2 tablespoons brandy
1 tablespoon vanilla
powdered sugar (for topping)

Beat egg yolks with electric beater until thick, gradually adding the sugar. Combine the zweiback, almonds, baking powder, cream of tartar, and orange rind, and add, mixing thoroughly. Add the brandy and vanilla and blend well. Beat the egg whites until stiff and fold into mixture. Pour into a very lightly greased 8-inch tube pan and bake at 350 degrees for 30 minutes. Cool before removing from pan, then sprinkle powdered sugar over it. Keeps well at room temperature if tightly covered. *Serves 12.*

RAVANI II

[Butter Almond Cake]

This version is from northern Greece.

¾ cup soft butter
¾ cup sugar
8 eggs

½ cup ground blanched almonds
1 teaspoon grated lemon rind
¾ cup farina
1 teaspoon baking powder
¼ teaspoon salt
½ cup Basic Syrup (page 177)

Cream together the butter and sugar with an electric beater. Add the eggs, one at a time, beating until very fluffy. Add the almonds and lemon rind and blend well. Combine the farina, baking powder, and salt, and add to the first mixture, mixing together very well. Pour into a well-greased 8x8x3-inch pan and bake at 350 degrees for 25 to 30 minutes. Leave in the pan to cool. When cool, pour warm syrup over it. Cut into diamond-shape pieces. Keeps a few days at room temperature. Do not refrigerate. *Serves 12.*

COCOANUT TOURTA

[Cocoanut Cake]

This is a recipe from a teacher in a homemaking school in Kastoria, Macedonia. The cocoanut is newly introduced to Greece and is known only by its English name.

½ cup soft butter
1 cup sugar
6 egg whites
1½ cups lightly packed grated cocoanut
1¾ cups sifted cake flour
½ teaspoon salt
2 teaspoons baking powder
¾ cup milk
1 teaspoon almond flavoring
¾ cup Basic Syrup (page 177)

Cream together the butter and sugar. Add the unbeaten egg whites and continue to beat until creamy. Stir in the cocoanut. Sift together the flour and salt and add to the mixture, mixing well. Dissolve the baking powder in the milk and add, mixing for just a minute. Blend in the almond flavoring. Pour into a lightly greased 8x10x2-inch pan and bake at 350 degrees for 40 minutes. Leave in the pan to cool. When cool pour warm syrup over it and allow to stand for two hours before slicing into squares. Keeps a few days at room temperature. Do not refrigerate. *Serves 12 to 16.*

YAOURTI, KARETHOPITA ME STAFITHES

[Yogurt, Walnut, and Raisin Cake]

This is a heavy cake, something like a fruitcake, which uses the most plentiful products of Greece.

1¼ *cups yogurt*
½ *cup sugar*
1 *cup farina*
2 *teaspoons baking powder*
¼ *teaspoon baking soda*
¼ *teaspoon salt*
¼ *teaspoon cinnamon*
1 *cup light raisins*
1½ *cups chopped walnuts*
1 *teaspoon grated orange rind*
¼ *cup brandy*
Basic Syrup (page 177)

Mix the yogurt and sugar together in a large bowl. Sift together the farina, baking powder, baking soda, salt, and cinnamon, and stir into the yogurt mixture. Wash the raisins and add, then add nuts, orange rind, and brandy, and mix together well.

Pour into a greased 7-inch tube pan and bake at 325 degrees for
1 hour. Cool before removing from pan, then pour warm syrup
over it. Keeps well at room temperature if tightly covered. Do not
refrigerate. *Serves 16.*

PITA AYIOU FANOUREO

[St. Fanoureo's Cake]

This cake is made as a Thanks Offering to Saint Fanoureo, the
patron saint of lost articles. The loser pledges a cake in his prayer
to the saint for the return of his lost article, and when the prayer
is answered with the finding of the article, this cake is taken to
the church for a blessing. It is then cut into nine pieces and distributed to the poor outside the church door.

1½ cups orange juice
½ cup cream sherry
2 tablespoons shortening
2 cups light raisins
1 cup sugar
1 teaspoon salt
1 tablespoon cinnamon
2 tablespoons brandy or rum
2 cups sifted all-purpose flour
1½ teaspoons baking powder
½ teaspoon baking soda
¾ cup chopped walnuts (optional)

In a saucepan combine orange juice, sherry, shortening, raisins,
sugar, salt, cinnamon, and liquor. Bring to a boil and cook for 10
minutes, stirring often. Remove from flame and cool.

Sift together the flour, baking powder, and baking soda, and
stir into the cooled mixture. Blend until smooth, then add the

nuts and mix well. Pour into a greased 7x3-inch tube pan and bake at 325 degrees for 1 hour and 15 minutes. Keeps well if tightly covered. *By tradition serves 9 but is enough to serve 16.*

COOKIES AND PUFFS

BASIC COOKIE DOUGH

This recipe makes a large quantity of dough which can be stored in the refrigerator for up to four weeks. It can be rolled out and cut into wafers with a cookie cutter or shaped in the hands into sticks. It is also used for the crust in Vissino Marenga (page 210) and Tarta Stafilia (page 212).

8 *cups sifted all-purpose flour*
1 *teaspoon salt*
4 *teaspoons baking powder*
½ *teaspoon baking soda*
1 *cup soft butter*
½ *cup shortening*
2 *cups sugar*
6 *egg yolks*
¼ *cup sour cream*
3 *tablespoons rum or brandy*
1 *tablespoon vanilla*

Sift together the flour, salt, baking powder, and baking soda. In another large bowl cream the butter, shortening, and sugar with a large wooden spoon. Add egg yolks and mix until creamy. Add sour cream, rum, and vanilla, and continue beating. Add dry ingredients, a cupful at a time, mixing well after each addition. Knead the dough until smooth.

For wafers, roll the dough thin, cut with a round cutter, and place on ungreased cookie sheet. Bake at 350 degrees about 12 minutes or until light brown.

For sesame sticks, roll dough with hands into small long rolls about size of little finger. Roll in sesame seeds and place on ungreased cookie sheet. Bake at 350 degrees 12 to 15 minutes. *Makes 18 dozen cookies or 4-eight-inch crusts.*

PISCOTA

[Tea Cookies]

This is a very old recipe for a cookie that is popular in city homes. It has poor keeping qualities so should be used within a few days.

5 *cups sifted cake flour*
1½ *teaspoons baking powder*
¾ *pound soft butter*
1¾ *cups sifted powdered sugar*
4 *egg yolks*
1 *cup ground blanched almonds*
2 *tablespoons brandy*
1 *egg white, slightly beaten*
¾ *cup chopped blanched almonds*
18 *maraschino cherries cut into quarters (optional)*

Sift together the flour and baking powder and set aside. In a large bowl cream together the butter and powdered sugar with an electric beater. Add the egg yolks and continue beating until the mixture is smooth and creamy. Add the almonds and brandy and mix until blended. Fold in the dry ingredients. The dough should be soft and pliable. Cut off small round pieces, dip in the egg white, then roll in the chopped almonds. Place on greased cookie sheet and flatten with fingers. A piece of maraschino cherry can be placed on top of each if desired. Bake at 350 degrees for 25 minutes or until light brown. *Makes 6 dozen.*

YAOURTI PISCOTA

[Yogurt Wafers]

2 *cups sifted all-purpose flour*
½ *teaspoon baking powder*
¼ *teaspoon baking soda*
¼ *teaspoon salt*
⅓ *cup soft butter*
⅓ *cup sugar plus 1 tablespoon*
1 *egg*
1 *tablespoon yogurt*
1 *tablespoon ouzo or gin*
1 *teaspoon vanilla*
2 *tablespoons light cream*
dash of cinnamon

Sift together flour, baking powder, baking soda, and salt. In a
large bowl cream the butter and ⅓ cup sugar. Beat in the egg,
yogurt, liquor, and vanilla. Beat until creamy, then blend in, a cup
at a time, the dry ingredients. Knead the dough until smooth. Roll
out thin and cut cookies with a round cutter. Place on a greased
cookie sheet. Mix together the cream, remaining sugar, and the
cinnamon, and brush over tops of cookies. Bake at 350 degrees
for 12 to 15 minutes or until golden brown. *Makes 3 dozen.*

COCOANUT PISCOTA

[Cocoanut Drops]

This is an Athenian party cookie.

3 *eggs, separated*
¾ *cup sugar*
8 *ounces shredded cocoanut*

1 *teaspoon almond flavoring or 1 jigger rose water*
9 *maraschino cherries cut in quarters (optional)*

Beat the egg yolks with electric beater until thick. Add the sugar gradually while continuing to beat. Add the cocoanut and flavoring and beat until all is blended well. Beat the egg whites until very stiff and fold into the mixture. Drop from a spoon in small balls onto a greased cookie sheet. Top each with a piece of maraschino cherry if desired. Bake at 325 degrees for 20 minutes. Remove from pan at once. *Makes 3 dozen.*

SKALTSOUNAKIA

[Cheese-filled Cookies]

This recipe is from a homemaking school in Neapolis, Crete.

PASTRY DOUGH:
6 *cups sifted all-purpose flour*
2 *teaspoons baking powder*
½ *teaspoon baking soda*
½ *teaspoon salt*
1 *cup soft butter*
1 *cup sugar*
2 *egg yolks*
¼ *cup yogurt*
2 *tablespoons rum*
1 *teaspoon vanilla*

FILLING:
2 *eight-ounce packages cream cheese*
2 *egg yolks*
½ *cup sugar*
1 *teaspoon cinnamon*
¼ *teaspoon salt*
1 *egg white, slightly beaten*

Sift together flour, baking powder, baking soda, and salt and set aside. In a large bowl cream the butter and sugar with a large wooden spoon. Add the egg yolks and continue beating. Add the yogurt, rum, and vanilla, and mix well. Fold in the dry ingredients, then knead until dough is soft. Cut off pieces of dough the size of a walnut, place on a greased cookie sheet, and press a well in center, fluting edge with thumb.

For filling, combine all ingredients except egg white in a bowl and beat with electric beater about 10 minutes. Fill centers of cookies. Brush tops with egg white. Bake at 350 degrees for 20 minutes. *Makes 4 dozen.*

KOURAMBIETHES

[Powdered Sugar Crescent Cookies]

This is one of the best-known Greek sweets and is served on all holidays.

1 pound butter
1 pound shortening
2 cups powdered sugar
2 egg yolks
3 tablespoons masticha* or gin
1 tablespoon almond flavoring
5 cups sifted cake flour
3 cups sifted all-purpose flour
1 pound powdered sugar (for coating)

Melt butter in a small saucepan, skim all the foam from the top, and carefully pour into a mixing bowl so sediment remains in bottom of pan. Melt the shortening and add to the melted butter. Gradually add the sugar while beating with electric beater, then

* Masticha is a Greek aperitif.

add egg yolks and beat until light and fluffy. Add liquor and flavoring and blend thoroughly. Sift together the cake flour and all-purpose flour. By hand fold in the mixed flour, a cupful at a time. Knead with the hands until dough is of right consistency to shape in hands without breaking. If too soft, add a little more all-purpose flour. Shape into crescents and bake on an ungreased cookie sheet at 350 degrees for 15 to 20 minutes. Do not overbake. While hot sprinkle with powdered sugar right on baking sheet. The cookies must be very cold before storing and they will stay fresh for several weeks. *Makes 80.*

MELOMAKAROUNA I

[Honey Mounds, Mainland Version]

These are very rich.

2½ *cups sifted cake flour*
2½ *cups sifted all-purpose flour*
¼ *teaspoon salt*
1 *teaspoon baking powder*
1 *cup butter*
1 *cup shortening*
1 *cup sugar*
2 *tablespoons orange juice*
1 *teaspoon rum*
1 *teaspoon vanilla*
2 *cups finely ground walnuts or pecans*
1½ *cups Basic Syrup (page 177)*
½ *cup powdered sugar*
1 *teaspoon cinnamon*

Sift together cake flour, all-purpose flour, salt, and baking powder, and set aside. Melt the butter and skim off the foam.

Transfer to a large bowl being careful to keep sediment in sauce-pan. Melt the shortening and add to butter. Gradually add the sugar while beating with an electric beater. Add orange juice, rum, vanilla, and half the nuts, and continue beating about 15 minutes. Fold in the dry ingredients, a cup at a time. Knead the dough until soft and pliable. Shape the cookies by rolling a teaspoonful of dough into an egg shape and squeezing it nearly flat in palm of hand with fingers of same hand. Arrange on an ungreased cookie sheet and bake at 350 degrees for 15 minutes or until light brown.

In the meantime prepare the syrup. In a small bowl mix to-gether remaining nuts, powdered sugar, and cinnamon. After the Melomakarounas have cooled, dip them, one at a time, in warm syrup and put on a plate to drain. Then transfer to a clean plate and sprinkle with the mixture of nuts, powdered sugar, and cin-namon. *Makes 3 dozen large or 6 dozen tea size.*

MELOMAKAROUNA II

[Honey Mounds, Island Version]

This is not as rich or sweet as the Mainland Version. Vegetable oil rather than shortening is recommended here.

¾ cup vegetable oil
¾ cup sugar
1 tablespoon honey
½ cup milk
1 tablespoon baking powder
¼ cup water
juice of 1 orange
¼ cup brandy
1 tablespoon cinnamon
¼ teaspoon salt

6 cups sifted all-purpose flour
1½ cups Basic Syrup (page 177), optional

In a large bowl cream together the oil, sugar, and honey. Slowly add the milk while continuing to stir mixture. Dissolve the baking powder in the water and stir into mixture, then add orange juice, brandy, cinnamon, and salt, and mix well. Fold in the sifted flour, a cupful at a time. Knead the dough until very smooth. To shape cookies, take a piece of dough the size of a walnut and roll in hand to the shape of a crescent. Place on a slightly greased cookie sheet and gently press tops with a fork to flatten slightly. Bake at 350 degrees about 15 minutes or until light brown. When cool dip in warm syrup (if desired) and place on a plate to drain. *Makes 4 dozen.*

KOULOURAKIA

[Easter Cookies]

These are served everywhere in Greece, especially from Easter Day until Ascension Day. They are shaped like the Sweet Bread Rings (Chap. 11), also known as Koulourakia, but are much smaller.

7 cups sifted all-purpose flour
1 teaspoon salt
4 teaspoons baking powder
½ teaspoon baking soda
1¼ cups soft butter
1½ cups sugar
5 egg yolks
2 tablespoons sour cream
2 tablespoons rum
1 tablespoon vanilla

1 teaspoon grated lemon rind
light cream (for brushing tops)
1½ cups sesame seeds

Sift together the flour, salt, baking powder, and baking soda, and set aside. In a large bowl cream together the butter and sugar, then add the egg yolks, one at a time, continuing to beat with a large spoon. Add the sour cream, rum, vanilla, and lemon rind, and mix well. Stir in the dry ingredients, then mix with hands and knead until the dough is soft and pliable. Cut off pieces the size of a small lemon, roll between hands to a 3-inch length, then twist each into a doughnut shape. Brush with cream and dip in bowl of sesame seeds. Shake off surplus seeds and place on a greased cookie sheet. Bake at 350 degrees for 20 minutes. When cool place in tins to store. *Makes 6 dozen.*

THIPLES

[Deep-fried Dainties]

A village housewife in Arcadia passed along her recipe for this popular village sweet.

2 cups sifted all-purpose flour
½ teaspoon salt
½ teaspoon baking powder
1 tablespoon sugar
3 eggs plus 6 yolks
1 pint vegetable oil
1½ cups Basic Syrup (page 177)
1 cup ground walnuts
1 cup powdered sugar
1 tablespoon cinnamon

Sift together the flour, salt, baking powder, and sugar. Beat the eggs and yolks until creamy and light in color. Add 2 tablespoons of the oil, mixing well, then fold in the dry ingredients. Rub the hands with oil and knead the dough for about 10 minutes until satin smooth. Place in a bowl, cover, and allow to stand for one hour.

In a deep heavy saucepan or deep-fryer heat the remaining oil to sizzling. Cut off a piece of dough about the size of an orange. With a rolling pin roll out to paper thin. Use a sharp knife or fluting wheel to cut strips about 2 inches wide and 12 inches long. Tie each in a loop. Drop into the hot oil and fry for just a few minutes, turning with a fork to brown evenly. Remove and place on paper towels to drain. Continue with remainder of dough. When cool, dip individually in warm syrup, being careful not to break, as they are very crisp. Mix together the ground walnuts, powdered sugar, and cinnamon and sprinkle over each piece. *Makes 4 dozen.*

SVINGOUS

[Fried Sweet Puffs]

These are traditionally served on Cheese Fare Sunday, the last day before Lent.

1 cup water
¼ cup butter
1 cinnamon stick
¼ teaspoon salt
1 cup sifted all-purpose flour
3 eggs
2 cups vegetable oil
¾ cup Basic Syrup (page 177)
¼ cup ground walnuts
¼ cup powdered sugar
1 teaspoon cinnamon

In a saucepan combine the water, butter, cinnamon stick, and salt, and boil 2 minutes. Remove the cinnamon stick. Add the sifted flour while stirring vigorously. Cook the mixture until it forms a gummy mass, pulling away from the side of the pan. Cool, then add the eggs, one at a time, beating with a spoon until very smooth. Heat the oil to sizzling in a heavy saucepan and drop spoonfuls of dough into the hot oil. Lower the heat a little and fry 5 to 7 minutes to golden brown. Drain on paper towels, then dip in syrup and place on a platter. Sprinkle a mixture of nuts, powdered sugar, and cinnamon over them. Serve immediately while still hot. *Makes 12.*

LALANGITES

[Rich Sweet Puffs]

This deep-fried and coated sweet is served by Macedonians to celebrate the birth of a baby.

4 eggs
¼ cup sugar
2 cups milk
2 yeast cakes
¼ cup lukewarm water
1 teaspoon salt
7 cups sifted all-purpose flour
1 pint vegetable oil
1½ cups Basic Syrup (page 177)
1 cup ground walnuts
1 cup powdered sugar
1 tablespoon cinnamon

Beat eggs well with electric beater, then add sugar gradually, continuing to beat. Pour in the milk, a little at a time, while beating at low speed. Dissolve the yeast in the lukewarm water and stir into the mixture. Combine salt and flour, add to mixture, and mix thoroughly. Cover the bowl with a cloth and put in a warm place to rise for 2 hours or until double in bulk.

In a deep heavy saucepan or deep-fryer heat the vegetable oil to sizzling. Scoop teaspoonfuls of the dough and drop into the hot oil. Fry a few minutes until the dough puffs up and turns golden brown. Drain on paper towels. Mix together ground walnuts, powdered sugar, and cinnamon. While still warm dip in cold syrup and roll in nut mixture to coat well. *Makes about 4 dozen.*

LOUKOUMADES

[Lenten Sweet Puffs]

This is one of the oldest Greek sweets, made everywhere in Greece through the winter and spring months right up to Ascension Day, but it is particularly associated with the Day of Forty Martyrs, March 9.

1 yeast cake
2 teaspoons sugar
1½ cups lukewarm water
4 cups sifted all-purpose flour
1 teaspoon salt
1 pint vegetable oil
1 cup Basic Syrup (page 177)
⅔ cup ground walnuts
⅔ cup powdered sugar
2 teaspoons cinnamon

Crumble the yeast cake in a large bowl, sprinkle with sugar, and let stand for 10 minutes. Pour ¾ cup of the lukewarm water over the yeast and stir to dissolve. Sift together the flour and salt and add 1½ cups of it to yeast and water. Mix with a large spoon until smooth, then cover the bowl with a cloth and put in a warm place to rise for 3 hours. The dough will look bubbly. Add the balance of the water and flour, mixing with a spoon. Rub the hands with a little oil and knead the dough about 10 minutes. Cover and put in a warm place to rise for 2½ hours or until double in size.

Heat the oil to sizzling in a deep heavy pan or deep-fryer. Drop in spoonfuls of dough and fry 5 to 7 minutes to a golden brown. Drain on paper towels, dip in cool syrup, and coat with mixture of nuts, powdered sugar, and cinnamon. Serve immediately while still hot. *Makes 40.*

PUDDING-TYPE DESSERTS

KASTANO FOLIA

[Chestnut Nests]

1 pound chestnuts
1½ cups milk
3 tablespoons sugar
dash of salt
1¼ cups heavy cream
1 teaspoon vanilla
6 maraschino cherries

Drop chestnuts in boiling water and cook until skins crack open. Cool slightly and peel. Heat the milk until warm, add chestnuts, 2 tablespoons of sugar, and the salt, and simmer until all milk is absorbed. Remove from flame and cool. Grind chestnuts in food chopper. Add ¼ cup cream and the vanilla and mash until very smooth. With a pastry tube shape the chestnut mixture into nests on dessert plates, starting with a circle and building it up in height but leaving a hollow center. Whip the remaining cup of cream and sweeten it with remaining tablespoon sugar. Fill the center of nests with whipped cream and top with a maraschino cherry. *Serves 6.*

HALVAH

[Fried Pudding Mold]

The recipe for this dessert, which is of Turkish origin, comes from the Peloponnesus. It is a heavy sweet, made in Greece with olive oil, but Americans will prefer it with vegetable oil or butter (much richer).

3½ cups sugar
4 cups water
1 cup vegetable oil or butter
1 cup farina
1 cup sifted all-purpose flour
1 cup chopped blanched almonds
1 teaspoon cinnamon

In a small saucepan combine 3 cups sugar and the water and boil for 10 minutes to make a syrup. Meanwhile heat the butter or oil in a heavy skillet. When very hot, slowly add the farina and flour, stirring constantly until it becomes brown, but being careful not to let it burn. Slowly add the syrup, stirring vigorously to prevent lumps from forming. Cook until all the syrup is absorbed. Add the almonds and pour into a 7-inch tube pan to mold. When it has set for 1 to 2 hours and cooled, remove to a plate and sprinkle with mixture of remaining ½ cup sugar and the cinnamon. *Makes 24 slices.*

KREMA KARAMALE

[Caramel Custard]

This is a popular dessert in all Mediterranean countries.

1 cup sugar
1 tablespoon water
3 cups milk
4 eggs
pinch of salt
1 tablespoon vanilla

Place 6 warm custard cups in a baking pan with hot water in the bottom. Combine ½ cup of the sugar and the water in a small heavy pan and cook over high heat, stirring constantly, until sugar caramelizes to a golden brown. Lift from heat immediately and spoon into bottom of warm custard cups. Warm the milk in a saucepan. Beat the eggs and add to milk with remaining sugar, salt, and vanilla. Mix well, then pour into cups over the caramel sauce. Place the pan of hot water with custard cups in 325-degree oven and bake 45 minutes or until knife inserted in custard comes out clean. Cool, then refrigerate for several hours before serving. *Serves 6.*

MELI PITA

[Honey Pie]

This recipe is from the island of Sifnos in the Cyclades, where it is a traditional dessert for Christmas and Easter.

PASTRY DOUGH:
1½ cups sifted all-purpose flour
1½ teaspoons baking powder

½ teaspoon salt
2 tablespoons sugar
½ cup butter
cold water

FILLING:
3 eight-ounce packages cream cheese
¾ cup sugar
2 teaspoons cinnamon
1 cup honey
6 eggs

Sift together the dry ingredients for pastry, then cut in butter. Add just enough cold water to make a soft dough. Knead the dough gently and roll out thin. Line a deep 10-inch pie pan with the pastry dough.

In a mixing bowl beat together the cheese, sugar, and half the cinnamon. Blend in the honey, then the eggs, one at a time, continuing to beat until very creamy. Pour the mixture into the lined pie pan and bake at 325 degrees for 45 minutes. Increase oven temperature to 375 degrees and bake 15 minutes longer or until light brown. Remove from oven and sprinkle remaining cinnamon over the top. Cool before serving. *Serves 12.*

RIZOGALO

[Rice Pudding]

This is the most popular family dessert in both the villages and the cities.

4 cups milk
⅓ cup rice
½ teaspoon salt

rind of ½ lemon, grated
2 eggs plus 2 yolks
⅓ cup sugar
1 teaspoon vanilla
cinnamon (for topping)

Heat the milk in a large saucepan to boiling. Add the rice and salt, cover, and boil gently for 15 to 18 minutes until rice is cooked. Add lemon rind. In a bowl beat the eggs well and slowly add the sugar while continuing to beat. Add to the rice and milk and cook 5 minutes longer, stirring constantly as it thickens. Remove from flame and add vanilla, stirring in well. Pour into sherbet glasses and sprinkle tops with cinnamon. Chill before serving. *Serves 6.*

FRUIT DESSERTS

MEELO PITA

[Apple Pie]

This Greek version of apple pie is found in many sweet shops in Greece.

PASTRY DOUGH:
2 cups sifted all-purpose flour
2 tablespoons sugar
1 teaspoon salt
½ cup soft butter
6 tablespoons cold water

FILLING:
5 cups grated cooking apples
1 cup sugar

¼ *teaspoon salt*
1 *teaspoon cinnamon*
1 *tablespoon sherry*

MERINGUE:
3 *egg whites*
6 *tablespoons sugar*
1 *teaspoon vanilla*
1 *teaspoon lemon rind*
1 *teaspoon lemon juice*

To make pastry dough, sift flour, sugar, and salt together. Work in the butter, then add water. Mix together, then knead to blend evenly. Roll half the dough to line the bottom of a 9-inch pie tin. Roll other half for top crust.

Mix together all ingredients for filling and spread over bottom crust. Cover with upper crust. Bake at 400 degrees until crust is light brown.

Beat the egg whites until stiff. In small amounts add the sugar, then vanilla, lemon rind, and juice while continuing to beat. Cover top crust with meringue, put in 400-degree oven, and bake about 5 minutes or until meringue is slightly brown. *Serves 6 to 8.*

MEELA SVINGA

[Apple Fritters]

6 *large cooking apples*
1 *cup sugar*
1 *cup water*
juice of ½ lemon
1 *ounce red cinnamon candy*
1½ *cups vegetable oil*

COATING:

3 *egg whites*
¼ *cup sugar*
¼ *cup beer*
¼ *cup sifted all-purpose flour*
¼ *teaspoon salt*

Peel, core, and quarter apples. In a saucepan combine sugar, water, and lemon juice. Bring to a boil, add apples, and cook about 10 minutes until apples are cooked through but still firm. Remove apples and drain in a colander. Add the cinnamon candy to the syrup and continue cooking until syrup is slightly thick.

To make coating, beat the egg whites until they begin to foam, then gradually add the sugar while continuing to beat. Add the beer, flour, and salt and beat until very smooth.

Heat the oil in a deep heavy saucepan or deep-fry pan to sizzling. Dip each apple piece in the coating and deep-fry until light brown in color. Place on paper towels to drain. When cool place the apples on a deep platter and pour the hot syrup over them. *Serves 6 to 8.*

KOUPES

[Fruit Tarts]

This recipe comes from a homemaking school in Neapolis, Crete.

1 *cup soft butter*
¾ *cup sugar*
2 *eggs*
1 *teaspoon grated lemon rind*
1 *teaspoon vanilla*
2½ *cups sifted all-purpose flour*
1 *teaspoon baking soda*

½ *teaspoon salt*
apricot, peach, cherry, or strawberry jam (commercial or from
  recipes in Chapter 13)

TOPPING:
4 eggs, separated
1 cup sugar
1 teaspoon grated lemon rind
1 tablespoon brandy or rum
1 cup ground almonds

Cream the butter and sugar by hand. Blend in the eggs, lemon rind, and vanilla. Sift together the flour, baking soda, and salt and add to the batter, blending in well. Knead the dough until smooth. Using greased cupcake pans or miniature tart pans, line bottoms and sides with a thin layer of dough, pressing it evenly with the fingers. Fill each tart with 2 teaspoons of jam.

Beat the egg whites until stiff, then add the egg yolks one at a time, continuing to beat. Add sugar, lemon rind, and liquor, and beat a little more. Add almonds and beat enough to blend. Put 2 or 3 spoonfuls on each tart. Bake at 350 degrees 30 to 35 minutes. *Makes 3 dozen.*

PASTA FLORA

[Fruit Squares]

These are cut into very small squares to be served at formal teas in Athens.

FILLING:
1 No. 2 can apricot halves, with juice
¾ *cup peach jam*
juice of ½ orange
juice of ½ lemon
2 tablespoons dry sherry
5 teaspoons cornstarch

PASTRY DOUGH:
⅓ *cup soft butter*
½ *cup sugar*
1 *egg*
½ *teaspoon grated orange rind*
1 *tablespoon brandy*
1 *teaspoon vanilla*
2 *cups sifted all-purpose flour*
1 *teaspoon baking powder*
¼ *teaspoon salt*

Drain apricots and retain ¼ cup juice. Combine apricots, peach jam, orange juice, lemon juice, and sherry in a saucepan. Dissolve the cornstarch in the apricot juice and add. Cook over a low flame, stirring frequently, until mixture thickens. Cool before spreading on pastry.

Cream together the butter and sugar with a large wooden spoon, then add the egg and mix until creamy. Add the orange rind, brandy, and vanilla, and blend. Sift together the flour, baking powder, and salt. Add the dry ingredients to the first mixture and knead until smooth.

Grease an 11x7x1-inch pan. Using half the dough, press it with the hands to cover the bottom of the pan. Spread the filling over the dough. In the hands roll the balance of the dough in strips for a lattice crust over the filling. Bake at 350 degrees for 40 minutes or until brown. *Makes 16 small pieces.*

VISSINO MARENGA

[Sour Cherry Meringue]

Basic Cookie Dough (page 190)
2 No. 303 cans sour red pitted cherries, with juice
2 tablespoons cornstarch
2 cups sugar

juice of 1 small lemon
1 envelope gelatine
½ teaspoon almond flavoring
few drops red food coloring

MERINGUE:

4 egg whites
½ cup sugar
¼ cup water
1 cup corn syrup
few drops lemon juice
1 teaspoon vanilla

Grease, then line a deep 8-inch round Pyrex pie dish with Basic Cookie Dough, pressing it thin to fit bottom and sides of dish. Roll long strips between the hands to press on rim, making a fluted edge. Prick the dough with a fork to make air holes over entire surface. Bake at 400 degrees 15 to 20 minutes or until light brown. Set aside to cool.

Drain juice from the canned cherries. Dissolve the cornstarch in half the juice and combine in a saucepan with sugar and lemon juice. Bring to a boil, stir until sugar is dissolved, then add the cherries. Soften the gelatine in balance of cherry juice and add to saucepan. Cook a few minutes until gelatine is thoroughly dissolved. Remove from flame, add flavoring and food coloring, and set aside to cool.

With electric beater beat egg whites until they form stiff peaks. Combine sugar and water in a saucepan and boil until thick, then add corn syrup and continue boiling until syrup spins a thread from a spoon. Pour the hot syrup very slowly into the beaten egg whites while beating them constantly. Add a few drops of lemon juice and continue beating until glossy. Remove from beater and fold in vanilla.

Pour the cooled cherry filling into the pie shell. Spread the meringue topping to cover it completely. Place in refrigerator for about 10 hours to set firmly. *Serves 10.*

TARTA STAFILIA

[Fresh Grape Tart]

This is similar to the preceding recipe for Vissino Marenga, but it has a different filling.

Basic Cookie Dough (page 190)
2 tablespoons cornstarch
½ cup lemon juice
½ cup orange juice
3 cups apricot nectar
1 cup sugar
1 envelope gelatine
¼ cup water
1 pound white seedless grapes or peeled and seeded red grapes
meringue (see Vissino Marenga, page 210)

Prepare dough and line an 8-inch pie dish as for Vissino Marenga. After baking set aside to cool.

In a saucepan combine the cornstarch with a little juice to make a smooth paste. Add the lemon juice, orange juice, apricot nectar, and sugar. Cook over medium flame, stirring constantly, for about 10 minutes until slightly thick. Soften the gelatine in water and stir into hot mixture, blending well. Set aside to cool.

Pour half of the cooled filling into the baked pie shell. Arrange the grapes in an even layer over filling and cover with remaining filling. Chill in refrigerator at least 6 hours.

Cover with cool meringue and chill again before serving. *Serves 10.*

PRESERVES
AND CANDIES

PRESERVES:

SEEKA GLYKO *[Fig Preserves]*
MEELO GLYKO *[Apple Preserves]*
ROTHAKENA GLYKO *[Peach Preserves]*
KYDONI GLYKO *[Quince Preserves]*
AHLADI GLYKO *[Pear Preserves]*
VISSINO GLYKO *[Sour Cherry Preserves]*
KARPOUZI GLYKO *[Watermelon Preserves]*
TRIANTAFILO GLYKO *[Rose Petal Jam]*
PORTOCALOFLOUDA *[Orange Rind Preserves]*
PORTOCALE MARMALATHA *[Orange Marmalade]*

CANDIES:

TROUFES SOKOLATA *[Chocolate Balls]*
TROUFES PORTOKALE *[Orange Balls]*
TROUFES AMEGTHALOTES *[Almond Bells]*
SOKOLATES *[Chocolate Bells]*
PASTELI *[Sesame Bars]*

13 · Preserves and Candies

CREEKS ARE fond of sweets, and often eat candy or glyko between meals. The abundant fruits of Greece are made into very sweet preserves they call glyko. As they have a more concentrated sweetness than most American jams and jellies they are not used in all the same ways. Marmalade is the only preserve generally used as a spread for bread or toast. Others are sometimes used as an ingredient in dessert recipes such as Pasta Flora, but the traditional way to serve glyko is as a "spoon sweet."

The preserve is served in a bowl on a silver tray along with a spoon, glass of water, and small glass of liqueur for each guest. Each person eats a spoonful of preserve, following it with a drink of water, then the glass of liqueur.

Glyko can be made from cherries, peaches, pears, apricots, figs, apples, quinces, seedless grapes, currants, berries, melons, citrus fruits and rinds, rose petals, and masteha gum, the last being used only for a beverage. Rose-petal glyko was an ancient medicinal preparation, but the marvelously flavored flowers of northern Greece have made it a sought-after delicacy.

There is always a little lemon and sometimes orange combined with the non-citrus fruits. The addition of sweet wine is often an improvement when preparing our domestic fruits, which may not be as full-flavored as those from the sunny Mediterranean. Almonds are a good addition to peach, pear, and quince preserves. Cloves and cinnamon pleasantly combine with many fruit flavors, but for something different, a sprig of sweet basil can be added to pears, or rose geranium can be added to quince. All the recipes given have been modified in sweetness to make them suitable for a variety of uses.

Many candies are made commercially in Greece, but home cooks use some of the abundant local products such as nuts, fruits, and honey along with imported chocolate for candy. Koufeta, the famous wedding candy of whole almonds with hard sugar coating, is usually made commercially. Loukoume, a gelatine candy of Turkish origin known to many as Turkish Delight, is made more successfully by professional candy-makers than by most home cooks.

The candy recipes we give are easy to make and some do not even require any cooking.

PRESERVES

SEEKA GLYKO

[Fig Preserves]

8 cups fresh figs
1 orange, sliced
2 lemons, sliced
juice of 1 lemon
4 cups sugar
1 cup water

Wash the figs, cut off the stems, and put in a large kettle with other ingredients. Let stand for 4 hours, then boil gently for 1 hour. Remove the figs and continue to boil the syrup gently with orange and lemon for 30 minutes or until it thickens. Add the figs and cook another 30 minutes. Pack in sterilized jars and seal. *Makes 4 pints.*

MEELO GLYKO

[Apple Preserves]

8 *large green cooking apples*
2 *cups sugar*
juice of 1 lemon
juice of 1 orange
¼ *cup sherry*
3 *cinnamon sticks*
5 *cloves*

Peel and slice the apples and put in a large kettle with other ingredients. Cook until the apples are just tender. Remove the apples and boil the syrup gently about 30 minutes or until thick. Return the apples and cook 5 minutes longer. Remove spices. Pack in sterilized jars and seal. *Makes 2 pints.*

ROTHAKENA GLYKO

[Peach Preserves]

The pits are cooked with the peaches to give added pectin and flavor.

8 *cups sliced peaches and pits*
6 *cups sugar*
juice of 2 lemons
juice of 1 orange

½ *cup sherry*
2 *cinnamon sticks*

Place the sliced peaches and pits in a large kettle with sugar, juices, and wine and let stand for 4 hours. Add the cinnamon sticks, bring to a boil, and boil gently for 30 minutes. Remove the peaches and continue boiling the syrup an hour or more until thick. Add the peaches and cook 15 minutes longer. Remove cinammon sticks. Pack in sterilized jars, putting several pits in each jar also, and seal. *Makes about 4 pints.*

KYDONI GLYKO

[Quince Preserves]

6 *cups quince (about 3 pounds)*
5 *cups sugar*
juice of 1 large lemon
4 *cups water*
sprig of rose geranium (optional)
½ *cup blanched almonds*

Wash, core, and peel the quince. Cut in quarters, then slice in thin strips. Place in a kettle and let stand for several hours to turn pink. Add the sugar, lemon juice, and water and boil gently about 2 hours until the quince is tender and the syrup has thickened. Drop rose geranium in for last 5 minutes of cooking. Remove from flame, add almonds, and remove geranium sprig. Pack in sterilized jars and seal. *Makes 2 pints.*

AHLADI GLYKO

[Pear Preserves]

6 *cups thinly sliced pears*
4 *cups sugar*
juice of 1 lemon

1½ cups water
½ cup blanched slit almonds

Combine fruit, sugar, and lemon juice in a kettle and let stand 1 hour. Add water and cook gently 30 minutes. Remove pears and continue cooking syrup until thick, about 1½ hours. Return the pears to kettle and continue cooking 10 minutes longer. Add the almonds. Pack in sterilized jars and seal. *Makes 2 pints.*

VISSINO GLYKO

[Sour Cherry Preserves]

10 cups sour cherries
12 cups sugar
juice of 1 lemon

Wash and pit the cherries. In a heavy kettle put 2 cups sugar, 2 cups cherries, and continue, alternating, until all are used. Over a very low flame gradually heat until sugar turns liquid, then bring to a boil and cook for 20 minutes. Skim the top, then remove the cherries. Continue to cook the syrup 1½ hours or more until thick, then return the cherries and add the lemon juice. Cook 15 minutes more. Pack in sterilized jars and seal. *Makes 6 pints.*

KARPOUZI GLYKO

[Watermelon Preserves]

10 cups watermelon rind
8 cups sugar
1 large orange
1 large lemon
juice of 1 lemon
10 cloves

Peel the green skin from the watermelon rind but leave some

of the red. Cut in very small strips. Cut the orange and lemon
into very small pieces. Put the rind, orange, and lemon in a large
kettle. Cover with the sugar, put on the lid, and let stand for 10
hours or overnight. Add cloves and bring to a boil. Skim, then
continue to boil gently with lid on until it thickens—about 3 hours.
Stir occasionally to prevent mixture from sticking to bottom. Remove cloves. Pack in sterilized jars and seal. *Makes 8 to 9 eight-
ounce jars.*

TRIANTAFILO GLYKO

[Rose Petal Jam]

Use the petals of the earliest roses of May or June, for they
are the most tender. Roses with the strongest fragrance will be
the most flavorful.

6 cups fresh rose petals, tightly packed
5 cups water
5 cups sugar
½ cup port wine
juice of 2 large lemons

Wash the rose petals, place in a kettle with the water, and
cook for 2 hours. Add the sugar, wine, and lemon juice and continue cooking for 1½ hours or until syrup thickens. Pack in small
sterilized jars and seal. *Makes 5 to 6 eight-ounce jars.*

PORTOCALOFLOUDA

[Orange Rind Preserves]

Lemon or grapefruit rinds are also preserved by these directions. These make very attractive garnishes.

12 large oranges with thick rinds
6 cups sugar
4 cups water

Wash the oranges, cut them in half, and squeeze the juice from them with a reamer. Cut the rind in one long continuous strip about ¼ inch wide. Roll it up tightly and with a needle and heavy thread go through the center of the roll and tie the ends of the thread together tightly. Put the rinds in a heavy kettle and cover with water. Boil them for 10 minutes, then pour off the water. Rinse in hot water, cover with more hot water, and boil another 10 minutes. Repeat a third time and continue boiling until the rind is tender.

In another kettle combine the sugar, water, and juice from the oranges. Boil 15 minutes or until it becomes a thin syrup, then add the rinds and cook about one hour until the rinds are transparent and the syrup is thick. Cool enough to be able to cut threads from rinds. Pack in sterilized jars and seal. *Makes 2 to 3 pints.*

PORTOCALE MARMALATHA

[Orange Marmalade]

6 large navel oranges
3 cups water
3 cups sugar

Peel skin from oranges in sections. Cut out fruit pulp, separating from inside membrane. There should be about 2 cups of pulp. Mash the pulp and remove seeds if any. Combine it with water and sugar in a large saucepan and cook until it begins to thicken. Slice the rind in slivers about 1 inch long. Put it in a saucepan, cover with cold water, and boil 5 minutes. Pour out the water, cover with hot water and boil 5 minutes longer. Repeat the process 2 more times, the last time cooking about 30 minutes until the rind is soft. Drain the rind thoroughly and add to the syrup. Cook 1 hour or until clear and thick. Pack in sterilized jars and seal. *Makes 2 pints.*

CANDIES

TROUFES SOKOLATA
[Chocolate Balls]

This is an old and well-known candy the Greeks consider a
luxury. It is sold in many sweet shops in Greece.

4 cups sweet milk chocolate
4 cups ground walnuts
2 cups ground pecans
1 cup ground almonds
2 cups powdered sugar
3 tablespoons warm cream
2 tablespoons rum flavoring
blanched almonds (for topping)

Cut up chocolate and place in a large bowl over hot water to
melt. When it is a soft smooth consistency, add the other ingredients. If it is too stiff to work, add a little more warm cream.
Roll into balls using a tablespoon of mixture for each. Top each
with half a blanched almond. *Makes 12 dozen.*

TROUFES PORTOKALE
[Orange Balls]

These are served at Carnival Time.

rind of 8 oranges
2½ cups sugar
1½ cups water
¼ cup orange juice

1 ounce sweet milk chocolate
2 tablespoons brandy
1½ cups ground walnuts
1½ cups ground almonds
chocolate cake-topping seeds

Soak the orange rind in cold water for 4 hours. Drain, place in a saucepan and cover with water. Boil the rind for 5 minutes. Drain and repeat this process twice, the last time boiling until the rind is very soft. Drain and squeeze in a colander. Grind the rind in a food chopper.

Combine the sugar, water, and orange juice in a saucepan and boil until it begins to thicken. Add the ground orange rind and cook for 5 minutes. Add the chocolate and brandy and cook 2 minutes longer. Add the nuts and cook another 2 minutes. Remove from flame and cool. Roll into balls using a teaspoonful of mixture for each ball. Roll the balls in chocolate cake-topping seeds until well coated. *Makes 4 dozen.*

TROUFES AMEGTHALOTES

[Almond Bells]

These are popular for name days and weddings.

1 pound blanched almonds, ground
1 cup powdered sugar
4 tablespoons light cream
powdered sugar (for coating)

Combine the ingredients and knead with the hands until very well blended. Shape into little bells and roll in powdered sugar. *Makes 2 dozen.*

SOKOLATES

[Chocolate Bells]

This is a Christmas candy.

1 pound sweet milk chocolate
1 pound shelled walnuts or pecans, ground
3 cups powdered sugar
4 tablespoons light cream
3 tablespoons rum or 2 tablespoons rum flavoring
powdered sugar (for coating)

Chop up chocolate and place in a bowl over hot water to melt. When it is a soft smooth consistency add the other ingredients and mix together well. Cool a little, then shape into little bells and roll in powdered sugar. *Makes 3 dozen.*

PASTELI

[Sesame Bars]

These are made on the island of Amorgas to be shipped all over the world. They are sold by many street vendors in Greece.
2 cups sesame seeds
1¼ cups honey

Toast the sesame seeds in the oven at 400 degrees for 10 minutes. Combine the toasted seeds and honey in a heavy saucepan and bring slowly to the hard-boil mark on a candy thermometer. This takes about 10 minutes and the mixture should be golden brown. Pour the hot mixture on a large bread board and flatten with a wooden spoon to a sheet about ⅛ inch thick. Cut into bars about 2x4 inches and wrap individually in wax paper or Saran Wrap. Store in air-tight tins. *Makes 15 to 18 bars.*

BEVERAGES

KAFES *[Greek Coffee]*

LEMONADA *[Fresh Lemonade]*

PORTOCALADA *[Fresh Orangeade]*

VISSINADA *[Sour Cherry Drink]*

SOUMATHA *[Chilled Almond Drink]*

MASTEHA GLYKO *[Gum Preserve Drink]*

PAGOMENOS HEMOS FROOTA *[Chilled Punch]*

ZESTOS HEMOS *[Hot Punch]*

PAGOMENE MAVRODAPHNE *[Mavrodaphne Cooler]*

ATHENIAN COCKTAIL

14 · Beverages

AFFABLE, pleasure-loving Greeks enjoy sharing like company in the coffeehouses, tavernes, and sidewalk cafés sipping wine, coffee, or a glass of ouzo with their confrères. Wherever there are Greek people there is an invitation to linger and sip.

The coffeehouses are strictly a man's world, but the ladies enjoy socializing too, and frequent the patisseries as well as Athens' sidewalk cafes. Escorted ladies are part of the evening crowd in the city tavernes.

Though the per capita consumption of beverages is high, the assortment is not extensive. Among soft drinks, lemonade and orangeade, both bottled in Greece, are the favorites. Popular summer drinks, especially in the homes, are Vissinada, a sour cherry drink, and Soumatha, made from almonds. An herb tea called faskomilo which comes from native plants is cheap and plentiful, but imported tea, being very expensive, is served only in the city homes of the more prosperous. Few people are in the habit of drinking milk, for only in the last decade has cow's milk been generally available. Most of the supply is goat's and sheep's milk which is more appealing when converted to cheese or yogurt. Water and wines are the only beverages served with meals, but Greek coffee is often served following the meal.

Greek coffee is essentially the same as Turkish coffee, for the Turks introduced this beverage to the Greeks in the fifteenth century. The coffee beans, imported mainly from Brazil, are ground in wooden hand mills to a pulverized state. The brew is made in a small brass coffee pot called a "breke" and served in demitasse cups. It cannot be made properly in large quantity. Brekes are made in 2-, 3-, or 4-cup sizes and can be purchased in Greek stores in this country.

Coffee is ordered to taste, for it is spoiled if sugar is added or if it is stirred after it is poured into the cup. It is strong and thick when served, but the unhurrying Greek lets it settle and sips it slowly. There is a fortune to be read from the residue in the bottom of every cup.

Coffee without sugar is called *sketo*, with medium sweetness, it is *metrio*, and very sweet coffee is *varie glyko*.

The grapes of Greece are made into a variety of apéritifs, wines, and brandy. Ouzo and masticha are popular apéritifs. Ouzo is made from alcohol of fine-quality white grapes with a light flavor of anise or licorice root added. It is colorless and clear but turns milky when mixed with water. It is usually served in a tall glass with water.

Ouzo has been a popular Greek drink for more than two centuries originating in Thessaly in 1750. It was exported to Italy in crates marked "Per USO All'estero," in Italian meaning, "for foreign use," and thus the word ouzo originated.

Masticha is a popular ladies' drink. Also made from alcohol of pressed grapes, it takes its name and flavor from the essence of flowers of a special gum tree that grows primarily on the island of Chios. Masticha is usually served in a small liqueur glass.

There is a wide variety of Greek wines—resinated, dry, sweet, and sparkling. The most distinctly Greek is retsina, a wine made from white grapes with resin from the pine tree added during fermentation. The pine flavor is pronounced, and one must usually acquire a taste for it. There is also a rosé resinated wine called kokineli.

With fish the Greeks often serve vermouth, dry sherry from Akhaia in the northwest Peloponnesus, and Santa Helena, a white wine from the Patras area. Santa Helena and Kamba are two popular white dinner wines. Rombola from the island of Cephalonia is a good rosé, and among the good red wines are Castel Danielis and dark Demestica. Excellent champagne comes from Akhaia and Tegeas in the Peloponnesus.

Mavrodaphne is an outstanding dark sweet wine from Patras and is often served with fruit after dinner. The island of Samos produces good light dessert wines. A good one is Samos Dux.

Brandy and cordials are served frequently, both after dinner and for a between-meal pause with a snack or sweet. Metaxa and VSOP brandy and Barbaresso cognac are Greek brands known world-wide. Many fruit liqueurs come from the island of Rhodes, bottled in attractive earthenware jugs, and are sold in many sweet shops.

Though the Greeks seem to drink a great deal, they take their alcohol in moderation, and it is rare to see an intoxicated Greek. They never drink without also having a bite to eat. From mythology they remember that Bacchus, the god of wine, had the feet of a billygoat. Wine is a pleasurable gift when used wisely, but excessive drinking can turn a man into a beast. If a man gets drunk in Greece he is not considered a Man, for the drink is stronger than he, so he cannot help but acquire the feet of a billygoat!

Among these people who thrive on festivals and pleasurable but restrained appreciation of good wine, the annual Wine Festival at Daphne is a climactic event. Held on the grounds of the famous old Byzantine church at Daphne, just a short distance north of Athens, the festivities of several weeks' duration during September and early October give a visitor an opportunity to sample the full range of the year's vintage. After paying a nominal admission fee, the wine is free, and with approximately sixty varieties offered, it is wise to take a tip from the natives—have something to eat along with the wine-sipping to avoid getting billygoat feet!

KAFES

[Greek Coffee]

1 demitasse cup of water
½ to 3 teaspoons sugar
2 teaspoons pulverized Greek coffee

Put the water in a brass "breke" and place over flame until it boils. Add the quantity of sugar desired, stir thoroughly, and bring to a boil again. Remove from the flame and add the coffee, stirring vigorously until completely dissolved. Return to the flame and bring to a boil. It will have a foam on top. Remove from the flame until the foam goes down. Repeat this procedure three times to insure good coffee. Do not stir or add cream. Pour carefully into a demitasse cup to preserve the thick foam on top. Serve immediately. *Makes 1 serving.*

LEMONADA

[Fresh Lemonade]

2½ cups sugar
7 cups water
juice of 8 lemons
rind of 2 lemons, cut in pieces
1 pint soda water

Combine the sugar and water in a saucepan and boil for 5 minutes. Add the lemon juice and rind and boil 5 minutes longer. Cool, then pour into a pitcher with soda water and ice. *Makes 10 eight-ounce glasses.*

PORTOCALADA

[Fresh Orangeade]

Follow directions for Lemonade using 6 oranges, 2 lemons, and rind of 2 oranges. *Makes 10 eight-ounce glasses.*

VISSINADA

[Sour Cherry Drink]

1 quart fresh sour cherries
½ cup water
about 6 cups sugar
2 tablespoons lemon juice

In a saucepan boil the cherries and water until a soft mash. Skim and strain the juice, then measure. Use 1 cup more of sugar than quantity of juice. Boil together until syrupy, then add lemon juice and cool. Pour in jars to store.

To serve, use 2 tablespoons syrup in a tall glass and fill with ice water and an ice cube. *Makes 2 pints of syrup.*

SOUMATHA

[Chilled Almond Drink]

In Greece this unusual drink is made from prepared concentrate available in bottles. It can be made by the following directions:

2 cups finely ground blanched almonds
3 cups sugar
3 cups water
1 tablespoon almond flavoring

Use a wooden bowl and wooden spoon to mash the almonds to a paste with 2 or 3 tablespoons water and 5 tablespoons sugar. Work it until very smooth. Combine the balance of the water and sugar in a saucepan and boil for 5 minutes. Add the almond paste and continue boiling 15 minutes longer. Cool, then strain in a cheesecloth bag. Add the flavoring and bottle for storage.

To serve, use 2 tablespoons Soumatha in a tall glass and fill with ice water. *Makes 2 pints of concentrate.*

MASTEHA GLYKO

[Gum Preserve Drink]

This glyko is used only for a beverage, never as a spoon sweet.

3 cups sugar
1½ cups water
1 egg white
juice of ½ lemon
2 teaspoons masteha (dried gum granules)

Put sugar and water in a heavy saucepan, add the unbeaten egg white and stir until it begins to boil. Then skim off all the foam. Boil the syrup until it makes a soft ball when dropped into a glass of cold water. Add the lemon juice and cool a little. Pulverize the masteha and set aside. Beat the syrup with an electric beater and gradually add the masteha. Beat until white and creamy. Store in small jars.

To serve, use a spoonful in a glass of water. The glyko is usually left on the spoon in the glass rather than being stirred and dissolved. *Makes 1 pint of glyko.*

PAGOMENOS HEMOS FROOTA

[Chilled Punch]

1 *pint Greek champagne*
1 *quart dry white wine*
1 *cup Metaxa brandy*
1 *quart soda water*
2 *large oranges, sliced*
1 *small can pineapple chunks*

Chill all ingredients before combining in punch bowl. Place the bowl in a pan of crushed ice or use a large chunk of ice in the punch bowl, but avoid diluting with melting ice. *Makes 3 quarts.*

ZESTOS HEMOS

[Hot Punch]

4 *cups hot tea*
1 *cup sugar*
juice of 8 oranges
juice of 3 lemons
1¼ *cups cognac*

Dissolve the sugar in the hot tea. Strain the orange and lemon juice and add, then add cognac. Serve hot in small punch glasses. *Makes 16 four-ounce glasses.*

PAGOMENE MAVRODAPHNE
[Mavrodaphne Cooler]

crushed ice
2 ounces mavrodaphne wine
soda water

Partially fill a tall glass with crushed ice. Add the wine, then fill glass with soda water. *Makes 1 serving.*

ATHENIAN COCKTAIL

4 ounces Metaxa brandy
4 ounces mavrodaphne wine
4 ounces sweet vermouth
2 to 3 dashes Angostura bitters

Put all ingredients in a cocktail shaker with crushed ice. Shake well and pour into small glasses to serve. *Serves 8.*

MISCELLANEOUS

LADO-LEMONO *[Oil and Lemon Sauce for Fish]*

SALTSA SAVORE *[Fish Sauce]*

SKORDALIA I *[Garlic Sauce]*

SKORDALIA II *[Garlic Sauce, Lenten Version]*

MAYONEZA *[Greek Mayonnaise]*

SALTSA DIA PSARIKA *[Seafood Sauce]*

SALTSA THIOSMO *[Mint Sauce]*

YAOURTI *[Yogurt]*

HILOPITES *[Greek Noodles]*

TRAHANA *[Pasta Meal]*

HOMEMADE PASTRY DOUGH

MACARONADA *[Macaroni with Cheese]*

METHESMENO RIZE *[Tipsy Rice]*

PSITA AVGA ME SALTSA *[Baked Eggs]*

AVGA ME RIZE *[Scrambled Eggs with Rice]*

TYROPITA I *[Cheese Pie]*

TYROPITA II *[Cheese Pie with Fillo Pastry]*

SPANAKOPITA *[Spinach Pie]*

SALTSA DIA PASTA *[Meatless Sauce]*

15 · Miscellaneous

TO COMPLETE this collection we must include a number of recipes which do not properly fall into the preceeding chapter classifications but are important to Greek cookery: the egg, cheese, and pasta dishes for meatless days; the sauces; and yogurt, the most important dairy food for Greeks.

LADO-LEMONO

[Oil and Lemon Sauce for Fish]

This recipe can be cut in half when ½ cup of sauce is required. Use it only when fresh.

½ *cup olive oil*
½ *cup lemon juice*
1 *teaspoon oregano*
½ *teaspoon salt*

Combine all ingredients in a covered jar and shake well. *Makes one cup.*

SALTSA SAVORE

[Fish Sauce]

1 tablespoon oil (in which fish was cooked)
1 cup tomato sauce
3 tablespoons dry white wine
juice of 1 lemon
1 tablespoon wine vinegar
2 cloves garlic, very finely chopped
1 teaspoon salt
1 teaspoon oregano
2 bay leaves, crushed

The sauce can be cooked in the same skillet in which the fish was fried. Combine all ingredients and cook, uncovered, over a low flame 15 to 20 minutes or until slightly thick. Pour over fish just before serving. *Makes about one cup.*

SKORDALIA 1

[Garlic Sauce]

This is served over boiled beets, fried eggplant, fried zucchini, codfish, fried squid and braised rabbit. It is most successful if made in a blender, but an electric beater is satisfactory if almonds are finely ground and garlic completely crushed with a mortar and pestle.

5 cloves garlic
3 small boiled potatoes, mashed
½ cup finely ground blanched almonds
¾ cup olive oil
juice of 1 lemon
1 tablespoon wine vinegar

2 *egg yolks*
1 *teaspoon salt*

Skin the garlic and crush thoroughly. Combine all ingredients in an electric blender or bowl and beat with electric beater until as smooth as mayonnaise. Can be stored in refrigerator one week. *Makes about two cups.*

SKORDALIA II

[Garlic Sauce, Lenten Version]

4 *cloves garlic*
6 *slices stale bread, without crusts*
1 *cup warm water*
½ *cup finely ground walnuts or pignolia nuts (pine nuts)*
1 *cup olive oil*
juice of 1 lemon
1 *teaspoon wine vinegar*
1 *teaspoon salt*

Skin the garlic and crush thoroughly. Soak the bread in water, then squeeze out. Combine garlic, bread, and nuts in a bowl. Add a little of the oil and beat together, then add balance of oil, alternating with lemon juice and vinegar until all is mixed. Add the salt and beat until sauce is very smooth. Can be stored in refrigerator one week. *Makes about 2 cups.*

MAYONEZA

[Greek Mayonnaise]

This is used with fish, boiled meats, and boiled chicken.

3 *egg yolks*
¾ *cup olive oil*
juice of 1 lemon

1 teaspoon salt
1 boiled potato, mashed

Beat the egg yolks until very thick. Add the olive oil in drops while continuing to beat. Add the lemon juice gradually, then salt and mashed potato. Beat until very smooth. This is best served fresh but can be kept in the refrigerator a week. *Makes about 1½ cups.*

SALTSA DIA PSARIKA

[Seafood Sauce]

This is a simple but tasty dip for boiled shrimp or any small fish.

4 tablespoons tomato catsup
4 tablespoons mayonnaise
1 tablespoon prepared mustard
dash of salt

Blend all ingredients together until smooth. *Makes ½ cup.*

SALTSA THIOSMO

[Mint Sauce]

1 cup fresh mint leaves
1 teaspoon wine vinegar
½ teaspoon powdered sugar
¼ teaspoon salt
dash of pepper
¾ cup hot water

Wash mint leaves and chop very fine. Combine them in a bowl with vinegar, sugar, salt, and pepper. Pour the hot water over mixture and let stand 5 minutes before serving over sliced meat. *Makes 1 cup.*

YAOURTI

[Yogurt]

Yogurt can be made at home by introducing yogurt culture into fresh milk, using a small amount of either commercially made or homemade yogurt from a previous batch as a starter. Under the proper conditions the bacteria multiplies, converting all the milk to yogurt. Keep it at a constant temperature just under 120 degrees for at least six hours. Higher temperature will kill the culture, and lower than 90 degrees will halt the bacteria action and cause it to turn sour.

1 quart homogenized milk plus ½ cup
2 tablespoons commercial yogurt

Scald the quart of milk, then allow to cool to 120 degrees. Use a candy thermometer to test temperature. Warm the ½ cup milk slightly and blend it with the yogurt until smooth. Add to the warm milk, cover, and let stand in a warm place for 6 hours. The temperature should be held above 100 degrees.

After 6 hours pour the yogurt into a muslin bag and hang to drain for 3 hours. Place in jars and keep refrigerated. Will keep 2 to 3 weeks. *Makes 1½ cups.*

HILOPITES

[Greek Noodles]

These should be made only during warm dry weather so there is no danger of molding.

12 eggs
1 cup milk
1 cup light cream
½ cup melted butter
1 tablespoon salt
12 cups flour (3 pounds)

In a large bowl beat the eggs, add milk, cream, melted butter, and salt, and beat together well. Add the flour and knead the dough until soft and pliable. If it seems sticky put a little vegetable oil on the hands and continue kneading to make very smooth. Cover with a cloth and let it stand for 9 hours. It may be convenient to make the dough in the evening and roll it out the next morning.

Cut off pieces the size of a large orange and roll out as thin as possible. Let it dry for a few minutes before cutting into thin strips. Cut the strips into small squares. Put the noodles on a large tray lined with a clean cloth and place in a sunny window to dry for 3 days. Stir them occasionally so all are evenly exposed to air and sun. Store in tins or a crock to use through winter. *Makes 5½ to 6 pounds.*

TRAHANA

[Pasta Meal]

This should be made only during warm dry weather so there is no danger of molding. It is used for soup and as a breakfast food. A covered earthenware crock is necessary for making this —an ordinary pan will not do.

1 pint milk
1 pint half-and-half cream
¼ cup salt
¼ cup butter
4 eggs
6 yeast cakes
½ cup lukewarm water
16 cups flour (4 pounds)
2 tablespoons vegetable oil

Pour milk, cream, and salt into an earthenware crock. Cover it and put in a warm place to remain for 12 days to sour. Do not stir it. If mold forms, skim off and discard.

In a very large pan combine the sour milk with butter, eggs, and yeast that is dissolved in lukewarm water. Add the flour and knead until dough is smooth. Rub the hands with vegetable oil and continue kneading for 20 minutes. Cover with a cloth and put aside for 14 hours. If it rises too high punch it down.

Spread a clean tablecloth out on a large surface. Separate the dough into pieces the size of a walnut and put them on the cloth to dry for several hours. Turn them so they will dry evenly. Rub the pieces over a grater to crumble all the dough so it resembles course meal. Place it on a large tray lined with a clean cloth. Spread wax paper over the meal. Leave it in a warm, dry place for a week, turning occasionally. Place it in direct sunlight for two more days, then store in tins for winter use. *Makes 4 to 4½ pounds.*

HOMEMADE PASTRY DOUGH

This dough can be used for any meat or cheese pie. It does not resemble fillo but can be used as a substitute except in dessert recipes.

1¾ cups sifted flour
1½ teaspoons baking powder
½ teaspoon salt
½ cup butter or margarine
⅓ cup water
3 tablespoons melted butter (for brushing dough)

Sift together the flour, baking powder, and salt. Cut in the butter and blend well. Gradually add the water while stirring to mix well. Turn out on a floured board and knead until smooth. Roll out very thin. Brush crust with butter when assembling pie. Follow recipe directions for baking. *Enough for 1 nine-inch pie.*

MACARONADA

[Macaroni with Cheese]

This dish is always served on Cheese Fare Sunday, the second Sunday before Lent. Greeks always use kefalotyri cheese, but one of milder flavor can be substituted.

1½ quarts water
1 tablespoon salt
½ pound macaroni
⅓ cup butter
1¼ cups grated cheese

Bring water to a boil, add salt and macaroni, and boil 15 minutes or until done. Pour off the water, rinse with scalding water, and place in a colander to drain. Heat the butter until it just begins to turn brown. Spread one third of macaroni on a platter. Cover with one third of the butter and one third of the cheese. Repeat for 3 layers. *Serves 4.*

METHESMENO RIZE

[Tipsy Rice]

This originated during the communist occupation when food supplies were short. Wine from hidden casks was cooked with rice to vary the monotonous diet. Then it was made only of water, wine, and rice.

1 cup water or meat stock
1½ cups port wine
1 teaspoon salt

1 cup rice
1 tablespoon oregano
2 tablespoons butter

Combine water or stock, wine, and salt in a saucepan and bring to a boil. Add the rice, cover, and boil gently for 18 minutes. Add the oregano and butter and mix well. *Serves 4.*

PSITA AVGA ME SALTSA

[Baked Eggs]

4 large slices salami
3 tablespoons grated kefalotyri cheese (or Parmesan or Romano)
4 eggs
salt and pepper
¾ cup tomato sauce
2 tablespoons cracker crumbs

Generously butter two individual-size Pyrex baking dishes. Cover bottom of each with 2 slices salami. Sprinkle half the cheese over meat. Break 2 eggs into each dish, being careful not to break yolks. Season tomato sauce with salt and pepper and spoon around eggs. Sprinkle cracker crumbs and remaining cheese on top. Bake at 400 degrees about 15 minutes or until eggs are firm. *Serves 2.*

AVGA ME RIZE

[Scrambled Eggs with Rice]

4 large very firm tomatoes
salt and pepper
sugar
½ cup cracker crumbs
⅓ cup vegetable oil

4 *tablespoons butter*
2 *large onions, grated*
8 *eggs*
½ *cup cooked rice*

Cut tomatoes in thick slices, sprinkle with salt and pepper and a little sugar, and coat with cracker crumbs. Heat oil in a skillet and fry tomatoes until brown on both sides. Drain on paper towels.

In a clean skillet melt the butter and sauté onions until golden. Beat the eggs in a bowl and add salt, pepper, and rice. Add to onions in skillet and stir from bottom as they cook over a low flame.

Place eggs and rice in center of a serving plate and surround with fried tomato slices. *Serves 4 to 6.*

TYROPITA I

[Cheese Pie]

4 *tablespoons butter*
1 *onion, grated*
1 *pound feta cheese, crumbled*
¼ *pound grated kefalotyri cheese*
1 *cup milk*
6 *eggs*
1 *tablespoon farina*
dash of cayenne red pepper
¼ *teaspoon finely ground dill*
¼ *teaspoon nutmeg*
Homemade Pastry Dough (page 243)

Melt 1 tablespoon butter in a small skillet and sauté onion. In a bowl mash the feta cheese. Add the other ingredients except remaining butter to the cheese and mix until fairly smooth. This will be a loose mixture.

Prepare the dough for crust. Roll half the dough to fit a 10-inch round Pyrex pie dish 1½ inches deep. Melt remaining butter and brush half of it over the crust, then cover with cheese mixture. Using balance of dough roll the upper crust and place over the cheese mixture. Press edges together around rim. Brush top with balance of butter and prick the top with a fork. Bake at 350 degrees for 1 hour or until knife inserted in center comes out clean. Serve warm. *Serves 12.*

TYROPITA II

[Cheese Pie with Fillo Pastry]

This is often served as a luncheon dish or the beginning course at dinner. See directions for handling fillo on page 176.

1 pound feta cheese
4 ounces cottage cheese (large curd, creamed)
3 eggs plus 3 yolks
2 tablespoons cream
dash of nutmeg
½ pound fillo
½ pound butter, melted

Blend together the feta cheese and cottage cheese. Add the eggs, cream, and nutmeg and blend well. Use half the fillo for the bottom crust in a pan 8x8x1½ inches. Brush each layer of fillo generously with melted butter. Spread the cheese mixture over the layers of fillo and use remaining fillo for top crust, brushing each layer with butter as before. Pour any remaining butter over the top. Score through the top layers of fillo in size pieces desired. Bake at 350 degrees for 1 hour. Serve hot. *Makes 12 large pieces or 20 small pieces.*

SPANAKOPITA

[Spinach Pie]

This is served as a luncheon dish or the beginning course at dinner. See directions for handling fillo on page 176.

spinach filling (see Spanakopitakia, page 33)
½ pound fillo
½ pound butter, melted

Prepare the spinach filling. Use an 8x8x1½-inch pan. Line the bottom with half the fillo sheets, brushing each generously with butter. Spread the filling over the fillo and cover with remaining fillo, brushing each layer with butter as before. Pour any remaining butter over top. Score through the top layers of fillo in size pieces desired. Bake at 350 degrees for 1 hour. *Makes 12 large or 20 small pieces.*

SALTSA DIA PASTA

[Meatless Sauce]

This is served with spaghetti, rice, or orzo. Oil is substituted for butter and no cheese is served over top if this is a Lenten dish.

⅓ cup butter
2 large onions, sliced
1 large green pepper, sliced
1½ cups canned tomatoes
½ cup tomato sauce
¼ cup dry red wine
1½ teaspoons salt
¼ teaspoon pepper
dash of sugar
1 tablespoon chopped parsley

Melt the butter in a large skillet. Add the onions and green pepper and sauté until soft. Add the other ingredients, cover, and cook over a low flame about 40 minutes until sauce is thick. Serve over hot spaghetti, rice, or orzo with grated cheese sprinkled over the top. *Serves 4.*

TABLE OF WEIGHTS AND MEASURES

All recipes in this book give ingredients in level measurements according to the following standard table:

dash or pinch = less than ⅛ teaspoon
1 teaspoon   = ⅓ tablespoon
1 tablespoon   = 3 teaspoons
1 fluid ounce   = 2 tablespoons
1 jigger   = 1½ ounces or 3 tablespoons
¼ cup   = 4 tablespoons
⅓ cup   = 5⅓ tablespoons
½ cup   = 8 tablespoons
1 cup   = 16 tablespoons or 8 fluid ounces
1 pint   = 2 cups
1 quart   = 2 pints or 32 fluid ounces
1 gallon   = 4 quarts
1 pound   = 16 ounces

APPROXIMATE CONTENTS
OF STANDARD CAN SIZES

Buffet = 1 cup or 8 fluid ounces
Picnic = 1¼ cups
#300   = 1¾ cups
#303   = 2 cups
#2   = 2½ cups
#2½   = 3½ cups

NOTES ON SHOPPING FOR
GREEK FOOD PRODUCTS

Most of the recipes in this book call only for standard ingredients available in any well-stocked grocery store. Imported Greek foods are available in many specialty shops. If you have difficulty locating them, we suggest you call the office of a Greek Orthodox Church in your community for shopping guidance.

If there is not a Greek Orthodox Church in your area, then there may not be any shops carrying Greek products. In this case you can order by mail, channeling your order through one of the large importing and distributing firms listed below, with the request that it forward the order to one of its retailers near you. Once your contact with a retailer is established, future ordering can be handled directly.

> George E. Athans Co.
>   160 Franklin Street, New York, New York
> N. Lekas Corp.
>   394 Greenwich Street, New York, New York
> Lekas & Drivas
>   98 Fulton Street, Brooklyn, New York
> Lekas & Drivas
>   809 West Randolph Street, Chicago, Illinois
> Moscahlades Bros., Inc.
>   30 North Moore Street, New York, New York

HOLIDAYS AND SPECIAL EVENTS
OF THE GREEK YEAR

The days marked * are national holidays in Greece. Where no date is given, the day is related to the date of Easter and is, therefore, a movable date. In the Greek Orthodox Church the date of Easter is calculated by the Julian calendar, so it often falls after the date celebrated by Western churches. Fixed dates in the Orthodox calendar conform with the Gregorian calendar.

* NEW YEAR'S DAY, January 1, traditional time for gift exchange.
  EVE OF EPIPHANY, January 5 (fast day).
* EPIPHANY, January 6, celebration of the baptism of Christ.
  CARNIVAL TIME, two weeks of festivity prior to beginning of Lent.
  MEAT-FARE SUNDAY, second Sunday before beginning of Lent, feast day during Carnival when lamb is traditionally served.
  CHEESE-EATING WEEK, second week of Carnival, when cheese and other dairy products are consumed before beginning of Lent.
  CHEESE-FARE SUNDAY, last day of Carnival, traditional day for serving cheese dishes, especially Macaroni and Cheese.
  GREAT LENT, 48-day period preceding Easter, period of religious observance and fasting, when meat, vertebrate fish, and all dairy and animal products are eliminated from the diet.
* CLEAN MONDAY, first day of Lent.
  CLEAN WEEK, first week of Lent, traditionally the time for spring housecleaning and whitewashing houses.
* INDEPENDENCE DAY, March 25, coincides with Annunciation Day; a slackening of the fast is allowed.
  PALM SUNDAY, sixth Sunday of Lent and one week befor Easter; fast is relaxed to allow serving of fish.
  HOLY WEEK, week preceding Easter, austere time of religious observance and stricter fasting when oil is also removed from the diet.
* GOOD FRIDAY, Friday preceding Easter, observance of Day of Crucifixion of Christ, with mourning and strict

fasting. The only food allowed is a special bean or lentil soup.

* EASTER SUNDAY, celebration of the Resurrection of Christ, the most festive celebration of the year.

* EASTER MONDAY, day following Easter, continuation of the Easter celebration.

ASCENSION THURSDAY, 40 days after Easter, end of Easter celebration.

* KING'S NAME DAY, Sts. Constantine and Helen, May 21.

* WHITE MONDAY, Feast of the Holy Spirit, Monday following seventh Sunday after Easter.

ALL SAINTS' DAY, eighth Sunday after Easter, celebrated as name day by persons not named for a particular saint.

SMALL LENT, August 1 to 15, fast period preceding Assumption Day.

TRANSFIGURATION DAY, August 6, fast relaxed to allow serving of fish.

* ASSUMPTION DAY, also known as Dormition Day, August 15, Feast of the Holy Virgin.

DAY OF BEHEADING OF JOHN THE BAPTIST, August 29 (fast day).

HOLY CROSS DAY, September 14 (fast day).

* OKHI DAY, October 28, holiday commemorating Greece's resistance to Axis attack in 1940.

CHRISTMAS FAST, November 15 to December 25.

* CHRISTMAS DAY, December 25, celebration of the Nativity of Christ.

* SECOND DAY OF CHRISTMAS, December 26, continuation of the Christmas celebration.

CALENDAR OF NAME DAYS

Most Greeks are named for saints of the Greek Orthodox Church. The day of the saint for whom a person was named is his name day and takes the place of his birthday as the occasion for annual celebration. A few name days fall during the time of Lent, but celebration of these is postponed until after Easter. All Saints' Day, the eighth Sunday after Easter in the Orthodox calendar, is celebrated as name day by all whose names are not derived from saints.

The following are the saint days most frequently celebrated by Greeks as name days:

January 1	St. Basil
January 7	St. John
January 17	St. Anthony
January 18	St. Athanasios
January 25	St. Gregory
February 6	St. Photios
February 8	St. Theodore
February 10	St. Haralampos
April 17	St. Thomas
April 23	St. George
April 25	St. Mark
May 5	St. Irene
May 21	Sts. Constantine and Helen
June 29	Sts. Peter and Paul
July 7	St. Kyriake
July 8	St. Theodosia
July 13	St. Gabriel
July 17	St. Marina
July 20	St. Elias
July 25	St. Ann
July 26	St. Paraskevi

July 27	St. Panteleimon
August 15	St. Mary
September 16	St. Euphemia
September 17	St. Sophia
September 20	St. Efstathios
October 5	St. Eudocia
October 11	St. Philip
October 18	St. Luke
October 20	St. Gerasimos
October 26	St. Demetrios
November 1	St. Cosmas
November 8	Sts. Michael, Gabriel, and Raphael
November 25	St. Catherine
November 26	St. Sylianos
November 30	St. Andrew
December 4	St. Barbara
December 5	St. Sabas
December 6	St. Nicholas
December 10	St. Mena
December 11	St. Daniel
December 12	St. Spyridon
December 15	St. Eleftherios
December 17	St. Dionysios
December 18	Sts. Sebastian and Zoe
December 26	St. Euthymios
December 27	St. Stephen

Index